C-910 CAREER EXAMINATION SERIES

This is your
PASSBOOK for...

X-Ray Technician

Test Preparation Study Guide
Questions & Answers

COPYRIGHT NOTICE

This book is SOLELY intended for, is sold ONLY to, and its use is RESTRICTED to individual, bona fide applicants or candidates who qualify by virtue of having seriously filed applications for appropriate license, certificate, professional and/or promotional advancement, higher school matriculation, scholarship, or other legitimate requirements of education and/or governmental authorities.

This book is NOT intended for use, class instruction, tutoring, training, duplication, copying, reprinting, excerption, or adaptation, etc., by:

1) Other publishers
2) Proprietors and/or Instructors of "Coaching" and/or Preparatory Courses
3) Personnel and/or Training Divisions of commercial, industrial, and governmental organizations
4) Schools, colleges, or universities and/or their departments and staffs, including teachers and other personnel
5) Testing Agencies or Bureaus
6) Study groups which seek by the purchase of a single volume to copy and/or duplicate and/or adapt this material for use by the group as a whole without having purchased individual volumes for each of the members of the group
7) Et al.

Such persons would be in violation of appropriate Federal and State statutes.

PROVISION OF LICENSING AGREEMENTS – Recognized educational, commercial, industrial, and governmental institutions and organizations, and others legitimately engaged in educational pursuits, including training, testing, and measurement activities, may address request for a licensing agreement to the copyright owners, who will determine whether, and under what conditions, including fees and charges, the materials in this book may be used them. In other words, a licensing facility exists for the legitimate use of the material in this book on other than an individual basis. However, it is asseverated and affirmed here that the material in this book CANNOT be used without the receipt of the express permission of such a licensing agreement from the Publishers. Inquiries re licensing should be addressed to the company, attention rights and permissions department.

All rights reserved, including the right of reproduction in whole or in part, in any form or by any means, electronic or mechanical, including photocopying, recording, or by any information storage and retrieval system, without permission in writing from the Publisher.

Copyright © 2024 by
National Learning Corporation

212 Michael Drive, Syosset, NY 11791
(516) 921-8888 • www.passbooks.com
E-mail: info@passbooks.com

PASSBOOK® SERIES

THE *PASSBOOK® SERIES* has been created to prepare applicants and candidates for the ultimate academic battlefield – the examination room.

At some time in our lives, each and every one of us may be required to take an examination – for validation, matriculation, admission, qualification, registration, certification, or licensure.

Based on the assumption that every applicant or candidate has met the basic formal educational standards, has taken the required number of courses, and read the necessary texts, the *PASSBOOK® SERIES* furnishes the one special preparation which may assure passing with confidence, instead of failing with insecurity. Examination questions – together with answers – are furnished as the basic vehicle for study so that the mysteries of the examination and its compounding difficulties may be eliminated or diminished by a sure method.

This book is meant to help you pass your examination provided that you qualify and are serious in your objective.

The entire field is reviewed through the huge store of content information which is succinctly presented through a provocative and challenging approach – the question-and-answer method.

A climate of success is established by furnishing the correct answers at the end of each test.

You soon learn to recognize types of questions, forms of questions, and patterns of questioning. You may even begin to anticipate expected outcomes.

You perceive that many questions are repeated or adapted so that you can gain acute insights, which may enable you to score many sure points.

You learn how to confront new questions, or types of questions, and to attack them confidently and work out the correct answers.

You note objectives and emphases, and recognize pitfalls and dangers, so that you may make positive educational adjustments.

Moreover, you are kept fully informed in relation to new concepts, methods, practices, and directions in the field.

You discover that you are actually taking the examination all the time: you are preparing for the examination by "taking" an examination, not by reading extraneous and/or supererogatory textbooks.

In short, this PASSBOOK®, used directedly, should be an important factor in helping you to pass your test.

X-RAY TECHNICIAN

DUTIES AND RESPONSIBILITIES
Under supervision, operates X-ray apparatus and auxiliary equipment, and develops negatives; may supervise subordinate personnel; performs related work.

EXAMPLES OF TYPICAL TASKS
Prepares and positions patients for taking X-ray pictures, according to standard procedures as prescribed by the physician in charge. Adjusts the X-ray equipment, operates controls to obtain correct exposures of films, in accordance with technical and safety standards. Labels film for identification and maintains required records. Maintains X-ray equipment in efficient operating condition, cleans apparatus and makes minor adjustments.

SCOPE OF THE WRITTEN TEST
The written test will be designed to test for knowledge, skills, and/or abilities in such areas as:
1. Radiologic procedures and radiographic techniques;
2. Radiographic exposure;
3. Anatomy, physiology systems and pathology;
4. Radiation protection and radiobiology;
5. Electrical and radiation physics; and
6. Related knowledge and skills.

HOW TO TAKE A TEST

I. YOU MUST PASS AN EXAMINATION

A. *WHAT EVERY CANDIDATE SHOULD KNOW*

Examination applicants often ask us for help in preparing for the written test. What can I study in advance? What kinds of questions will be asked? How will the test be given? How will the papers be graded?

As an applicant for a civil service examination, you may be wondering about some of these things. Our purpose here is to suggest effective methods of advance study and to describe civil service examinations.

Your chances for success on this examination can be increased if you know how to prepare. Those "pre-examination jitters" can be reduced if you know what to expect. You can even experience an adventure in good citizenship if you know why civil service exams are given.

B. *WHY ARE CIVIL SERVICE EXAMINATIONS GIVEN?*

Civil service examinations are important to you in two ways. As a citizen, you want public jobs filled by employees who know how to do their work. As a job seeker, you want a fair chance to compete for that job on an equal footing with other candidates. The best-known means of accomplishing this two-fold goal is the competitive examination.

Exams are widely publicized throughout the nation. They may be administered for jobs in federal, state, city, municipal, town or village governments or agencies.

Any citizen may apply, with some limitations, such as the age or residence of applicants. Your experience and education may be reviewed to see whether you meet the requirements for the particular examination. When these requirements exist, they are reasonable and applied consistently to all applicants. Thus, a competitive examination may cause you some uneasiness now, but it is your privilege and safeguard.

C. *HOW ARE CIVIL SERVICE EXAMS DEVELOPED?*

Examinations are carefully written by trained technicians who are specialists in the field known as "psychological measurement," in consultation with recognized authorities in the field of work that the test will cover. These experts recommend the subject matter areas or skills to be tested; only those knowledges or skills important to your success on the job are included. The most reliable books and source materials available are used as references. Together, the experts and technicians judge the difficulty level of the questions.

Test technicians know how to phrase questions so that the problem is clearly stated. Their ethics do not permit "trick" or "catch" questions. Questions may have been tried out on sample groups, or subjected to statistical analysis, to determine their usefulness.

Written tests are often used in combination with performance tests, ratings of training and experience, and oral interviews. All of these measures combine to form the best-known means of finding the right person for the right job.

II. HOW TO PASS THE WRITTEN TEST

A. NATURE OF THE EXAMINATION

To prepare intelligently for civil service examinations, you should know how they differ from school examinations you have taken. In school you were assigned certain definite pages to read or subjects to cover. The examination questions were quite detailed and usually emphasized memory. Civil service exams, on the other hand, try to discover your present ability to perform the duties of a position, plus your potentiality to learn these duties. In other words, a civil service exam attempts to predict how successful you will be. Questions cover such a broad area that they cannot be as minute and detailed as school exam questions.

In the public service similar kinds of work, or positions, are grouped together in one "class." This process is known as *position-classification*. All the positions in a class are paid according to the salary range for that class. One class title covers all of these positions, and they are all tested by the same examination.

B. FOUR BASIC STEPS

1) Study the announcement

How, then, can you know what subjects to study? Our best answer is: "Learn as much as possible about the class of positions for which you've applied." The exam will test the knowledge, skills and abilities needed to do the work.

Your most valuable source of information about the position you want is the official exam announcement. This announcement lists the training and experience qualifications. Check these standards and apply only if you come reasonably close to meeting them.

The brief description of the position in the examination announcement offers some clues to the subjects which will be tested. Think about the job itself. Review the duties in your mind. Can you perform them, or are there some in which you are rusty? Fill in the blank spots in your preparation.

Many jurisdictions preview the written test in the exam announcement by including a section called "Knowledge and Abilities Required," "Scope of the Examination," or some similar heading. Here you will find out specifically what fields will be tested.

2) Review your own background

Once you learn in general what the position is all about, and what you need to know to do the work, ask yourself which subjects you already know fairly well and which need improvement. You may wonder whether to concentrate on improving your strong areas or on building some background in your fields of weakness. When the announcement has specified "some knowledge" or "considerable knowledge," or has used adjectives like "beginning principles of..." or "advanced ... methods," you can get a clue as to the number and difficulty of questions to be asked in any given field. More questions, and hence broader coverage, would be included for those subjects which are more important in the work. Now weigh your strengths and weaknesses against the job requirements and prepare accordingly.

3) Determine the level of the position

Another way to tell how intensively you should prepare is to understand the level of the job for which you are applying. Is it the entering level? In other words, is this the position in which beginners in a field of work are hired? Or is it an intermediate or advanced level? Sometimes this is indicated by such words as "Junior" or "Senior" in the class title. Other jurisdictions use Roman numerals to designate the level – Clerk I, Clerk II, for example. The word "Supervisor" sometimes appears in the title. If the level is not indicated by the title, check the description of duties. Will you be working under very close supervision, or will you have responsibility for independent decisions in this work?

4) Choose appropriate study materials

Now that you know the subjects to be examined and the relative amount of each subject to be covered, you can choose suitable study materials. For beginning level jobs, or even advanced ones, if you have a pronounced weakness in some aspect of your training, read a modern, standard textbook in that field. Be sure it is up to date and has general coverage. Such books are normally available at your library, and the librarian will be glad to help you locate one. For entry-level positions, questions of appropriate difficulty are chosen – neither highly advanced questions, nor those too simple. Such questions require careful thought but not advanced training.

If the position for which you are applying is technical or advanced, you will read more advanced, specialized material. If you are already familiar with the basic principles of your field, elementary textbooks would waste your time. Concentrate on advanced textbooks and technical periodicals. Think through the concepts and review difficult problems in your field.

These are all general sources. You can get more ideas on your own initiative, following these leads. For example, training manuals and publications of the government agency which employs workers in your field can be useful, particularly for technical and professional positions. A letter or visit to the government department involved may result in more specific study suggestions, and certainly will provide you with a more definite idea of the exact nature of the position you are seeking.

III. KINDS OF TESTS

Tests are used for purposes other than measuring knowledge and ability to perform specified duties. For some positions, it is equally important to test ability to make adjustments to new situations or to profit from training. In others, basic mental abilities not dependent on information are essential. Questions which test these things may not appear as pertinent to the duties of the position as those which test for knowledge and information. Yet they are often highly important parts of a fair examination. For very general questions, it is almost impossible to help you direct your study efforts. What we can do is to point out some of the more common of these general abilities needed in public service positions and describe some typical questions.

1) General information

Broad, general information has been found useful for predicting job success in some kinds of work. This is tested in a variety of ways, from vocabulary lists to questions about current events. Basic background in some field of work, such as sociology or economics, may be sampled in a group of questions. Often these are principles which have become familiar to most persons through exposure rather than through formal training. It is difficult to advise you how to study for these questions; being alert to the world around you is our best suggestion.

2) Verbal ability

An example of an ability needed in many positions is verbal or language ability. Verbal ability is, in brief, the ability to use and understand words. Vocabulary and grammar tests are typical measures of this ability. Reading comprehension or paragraph interpretation questions are common in many kinds of civil service tests. You are given a paragraph of written material and asked to find its central meaning.

3) Numerical ability

Number skills can be tested by the familiar arithmetic problem, by checking paired lists of numbers to see which are alike and which are different, or by interpreting charts and graphs. In the latter test, a graph may be printed in the test booklet which you are asked to use as the basis for answering questions.

4) Observation

A popular test for law-enforcement positions is the observation test. A picture is shown to you for several minutes, then taken away. Questions about the picture test your ability to observe both details and larger elements.

5) Following directions

In many positions in the public service, the employee must be able to carry out written instructions dependably and accurately. You may be given a chart with several columns, each column listing a variety of information. The questions require you to carry out directions involving the information given in the chart.

6) Skills and aptitudes

Performance tests effectively measure some manual skills and aptitudes. When the skill is one in which you are trained, such as typing or shorthand, you can practice. These tests are often very much like those given in business school or high school courses. For many of the other skills and aptitudes, however, no short-time preparation can be made. Skills and abilities natural to you or that you have developed throughout your lifetime are being tested.

Many of the general questions just described provide all the data needed to answer the questions and ask you to use your reasoning ability to find the answers. Your best preparation for these tests, as well as for tests of facts and ideas, is to be at your physical and mental best. You, no doubt, have your own methods of getting into an exam-taking mood and keeping "in shape." The next section lists some ideas on this subject.

IV. KINDS OF QUESTIONS

Only rarely is the "essay" question, which you answer in narrative form, used in civil service tests. Civil service tests are usually of the short-answer type. Full instructions for answering these questions will be given to you at the examination. But in case this is your first experience with short-answer questions and separate answer sheets, here is what you need to know:

1) Multiple-choice Questions

Most popular of the short-answer questions is the "multiple choice" or "best answer" question. It can be used, for example, to test for factual knowledge, ability to solve problems or judgment in meeting situations found at work.

A multiple-choice question is normally one of three types—
- It can begin with an incomplete statement followed by several possible endings. You are to find the one ending which *best* completes the statement, although some of the others may not be entirely wrong.
- It can also be a complete statement in the form of a question which is answered by choosing one of the statements listed.

- It can be in the form of a problem – again you select the best answer.

Here is an example of a multiple-choice question with a discussion which should give you some clues as to the method for choosing the right answer:

When an employee has a complaint about his assignment, the action which will *best* help him overcome his difficulty is to
  A. discuss his difficulty with his coworkers
  B. take the problem to the head of the organization
  C. take the problem to the person who gave him the assignment
  D. say nothing to anyone about his complaint

In answering this question, you should study each of the choices to find which is best. Consider choice "A" – Certainly an employee may discuss his complaint with fellow employees, but no change or improvement can result, and the complaint remains unresolved. Choice "B" is a poor choice since the head of the organization probably does not know what assignment you have been given, and taking your problem to him is known as "going over the head" of the supervisor. The supervisor, or person who made the assignment, is the person who can clarify it or correct any injustice. Choice "C" is, therefore, correct. To say nothing, as in choice "D," is unwise. Supervisors have and interest in knowing the problems employees are facing, and the employee is seeking a solution to his problem.

2) True/False Questions

The "true/false" or "right/wrong" form of question is sometimes used. Here a complete statement is given. Your job is to decide whether the statement is right or wrong.

SAMPLE: A roaming cell-phone call to a nearby city costs less than a non-roaming call to a distant city.

This statement is wrong, or false, since roaming calls are more expensive.
This is not a complete list of all possible question forms, although most of the others are variations of these common types. You will always get complete directions for answering questions. Be sure you understand *how* to mark your answers – ask questions until you do.

V. RECORDING YOUR ANSWERS

Computer terminals are used more and more today for many different kinds of exams.
For an examination with very few applicants, you may be told to record your answers in the test booklet itself. Separate answer sheets are much more common. If this separate answer sheet is to be scored by machine – and this is often the case – it is highly important that you mark your answers correctly in order to get credit.
An electronic scoring machine is often used in civil service offices because of the speed with which papers can be scored. Machine-scored answer sheets must be marked with a pencil, which will be given to you. This pencil has a high graphite content which responds to the electronic scoring machine. As a matter of fact, stray dots may register as answers, so do not let your pencil rest on the answer sheet while you are pondering the correct answer. Also, if your pencil lead breaks or is otherwise defective, ask for another.

Since the answer sheet will be dropped in a slot in the scoring machine, be careful not to bend the corners or get the paper crumpled.

The answer sheet normally has five vertical columns of numbers, with 30 numbers to a column. These numbers correspond to the question numbers in your test booklet. After each number, going across the page are four or five pairs of dotted lines. These short dotted lines have small letters or numbers above them. The first two pairs may also have a "T" or "F" above the letters. This indicates that the first two pairs only are to be used if the questions are of the true-false type. If the questions are multiple choice, disregard the "T" and "F" and pay attention only to the small letters or numbers.

Answer your questions in the manner of the sample that follows:

32. The largest city in the United States is
    A. Washington, D.C.
    B. New York City
    C. Chicago
    D. Detroit
    E. San Francisco

1) Choose the answer you think is best. (New York City is the largest, so "B" is correct.)
2) Find the row of dotted lines numbered the same as the question you are answering. (Find row number 32)
3) Find the pair of dotted lines corresponding to the answer. (Find the pair of lines under the mark "B.")
4) Make a solid black mark between the dotted lines.

VI. BEFORE THE TEST

Common sense will help you find procedures to follow to get ready for an examination. Too many of us, however, overlook these sensible measures. Indeed, nervousness and fatigue have been found to be the most serious reasons why applicants fail to do their best on civil service tests. Here is a list of reminders:

- Begin your preparation early – Don't wait until the last minute to go scurrying around for books and materials or to find out what the position is all about.
- Prepare continuously – An hour a night for a week is better than an all-night cram session. This has been definitely established. What is more, a night a week for a month will return better dividends than crowding your study into a shorter period of time.
- Locate the place of the exam – You have been sent a notice telling you when and where to report for the examination. If the location is in a different town or otherwise unfamiliar to you, it would be well to inquire the best route and learn something about the building.
- Relax the night before the test – Allow your mind to rest. Do not study at all that night. Plan some mild recreation or diversion; then go to bed early and get a good night's sleep.
- Get up early enough to make a leisurely trip to the place for the test – This way unforeseen events, traffic snarls, unfamiliar buildings, etc. will not upset you.
- Dress comfortably – A written test is not a fashion show. You will be known by number and not by name, so wear something comfortable.

- Leave excess paraphernalia at home – Shopping bags and odd bundles will get in your way. You need bring only the items mentioned in the official notice you received; usually everything you need is provided. Do not bring reference books to the exam. They will only confuse those last minutes and be taken away from you when in the test room.
- Arrive somewhat ahead of time – If because of transportation schedules you must get there very early, bring a newspaper or magazine to take your mind off yourself while waiting.
- Locate the examination room – When you have found the proper room, you will be directed to the seat or part of the room where you will sit. Sometimes you are given a sheet of instructions to read while you are waiting. Do not fill out any forms until you are told to do so; just read them and be prepared.
- Relax and prepare to listen to the instructions
- If you have any physical problem that may keep you from doing your best, be sure to tell the test administrator. If you are sick or in poor health, you really cannot do your best on the exam. You can come back and take the test some other time.

VII. AT THE TEST

The day of the test is here and you have the test booklet in your hand. The temptation to get going is very strong. Caution! There is more to success than knowing the right answers. You must know how to identify your papers and understand variations in the type of short-answer question used in this particular examination. Follow these suggestions for maximum results from your efforts:

1) Cooperate with the monitor

The test administrator has a duty to create a situation in which you can be as much at ease as possible. He will give instructions, tell you when to begin, check to see that you are marking your answer sheet correctly, and so on. He is not there to guard you, although he will see that your competitors do not take unfair advantage. He wants to help you do your best.

2) Listen to all instructions

Don't jump the gun! Wait until you understand all directions. In most civil service tests you get more time than you need to answer the questions. So don't be in a hurry. Read each word of instructions until you clearly understand the meaning. Study the examples, listen to all announcements and follow directions. Ask questions if you do not understand what to do.

3) Identify your papers

Civil service exams are usually identified by number only. You will be assigned a number; you must not put your name on your test papers. Be sure to copy your number correctly. Since more than one exam may be given, copy your exact examination title.

4) Plan your time

Unless you are told that a test is a "speed" or "rate of work" test, speed itself is usually not important. Time enough to answer all the questions will be provided, but this does not mean that you have all day. An overall time limit has been set. Divide the total time (in minutes) by the number of questions to determine the approximate time you have for each question.

5) Do not linger over difficult questions

If you come across a difficult question, mark it with a paper clip (useful to have along) and come back to it when you have been through the booklet. One caution if you do this – be sure to skip a number on your answer sheet as well. Check often to be sure that you have not lost your place and that you are marking in the row numbered the same as the question you are answering.

6) Read the questions

Be sure you know what the question asks! Many capable people are unsuccessful because they failed to *read* the questions correctly.

7) Answer all questions

Unless you have been instructed that a penalty will be deducted for incorrect answers, it is better to guess than to omit a question.

8) Speed tests

It is often better NOT to guess on speed tests. It has been found that on timed tests people are tempted to spend the last few seconds before time is called in marking answers at random – without even reading them – in the hope of picking up a few extra points. To discourage this practice, the instructions may warn you that your score will be "corrected" for guessing. That is, a penalty will be applied. The incorrect answers will be deducted from the correct ones, or some other penalty formula will be used.

9) Review your answers

If you finish before time is called, go back to the questions you guessed or omitted to give them further thought. Review other answers if you have time.

10) Return your test materials

If you are ready to leave before others have finished or time is called, take ALL your materials to the monitor and leave quietly. Never take any test material with you. The monitor can discover whose papers are not complete, and taking a test booklet may be grounds for disqualification.

VIII. EXAMINATION TECHNIQUES

1) Read the general instructions carefully. These are usually printed on the first page of the exam booklet. As a rule, these instructions refer to the timing of the examination; the fact that you should not start work until the signal and must stop work at a signal, etc. If there are any *special* instructions, such as a choice of questions to be answered, make sure that you note this instruction carefully.

2) When you are ready to start work on the examination, that is as soon as the signal has been given, read the instructions to each question booklet, underline any key words or phrases, such as *least, best, outline, describe* and the like. In this way you will tend to answer as requested rather than discover on reviewing your paper that you *listed without describing*, that you selected the *worst* choice rather than the *best* choice, etc.

3) If the examination is of the objective or multiple-choice type – that is, each question will also give a series of possible answers: A, B, C or D, and you are called upon to select the best answer and write the letter next to that answer on your answer paper – it is advisable to start answering each question in turn. There may be anywhere from 50 to 100 such questions in the three or four hours allotted and you can see how much time would be taken if you read through all the questions before beginning to answer any. Furthermore, if you come across a question or group of questions which you know would be difficult to answer, it would undoubtedly affect your handling of all the other questions.

4) If the examination is of the essay type and contains but a few questions, it is a moot point as to whether you should read all the questions before starting to answer any one. Of course, if you are given a choice – say five out of seven and the like – then it is essential to read all the questions so you can eliminate the two that are most difficult. If, however, you are asked to answer all the questions, there may be danger in trying to answer the easiest one first because you may find that you will spend too much time on it. The best technique is to answer the first question, then proceed to the second, etc.

5) Time your answers. Before the exam begins, write down the time it started, then add the time allowed for the examination and write down the time it must be completed, then divide the time available somewhat as follows:
    - If 3-1/2 hours are allowed, that would be 210 minutes. If you have 80 objective-type questions, that would be an average of 2-1/2 minutes per question. Allow yourself no more than 2 minutes per question, or a total of 160 minutes, which will permit about 50 minutes to review.
    - If for the time allotment of 210 minutes there are 7 essay questions to answer, that would average about 30 minutes a question. Give yourself only 25 minutes per question so that you have about 35 minutes to review.

6) The most important instruction is to *read each question* and make sure you know what is wanted. The second most important instruction is to *time yourself properly* so that you answer every question. The third most important instruction is to *answer every question*. Guess if you have to but include something for each question. Remember that you will receive no credit for a blank and will probably receive some credit if you write something in answer to an essay question. If you guess a letter – say "B" for a multiple-choice question – you may have guessed right. If you leave a blank as an answer to a multiple-choice question, the examiners may respect your feelings but it will not add a point to your score. Some exams may penalize you for wrong answers, so in such cases *only*, you may not want to guess unless you have some basis for your answer.

7) Suggestions
    a. Objective-type questions
        1. Examine the question booklet for proper sequence of pages and questions
        2. Read all instructions carefully
        3. Skip any question which seems too difficult; return to it after all other questions have been answered
        4. Apportion your time properly; do not spend too much time on any single question or group of questions

5. Note and underline key words – *all, most, fewest, least, best, worst, same, opposite,* etc.
6. Pay particular attention to negatives
7. Note unusual option, e.g., unduly long, short, complex, different or similar in content to the body of the question
8. Observe the use of "hedging" words – *probably, may, most likely,* etc.
9. Make sure that your answer is put next to the same number as the question
10. Do not second-guess unless you have good reason to believe the second answer is definitely more correct
11. Cross out original answer if you decide another answer is more accurate; do not erase until you are ready to hand your paper in
12. Answer all questions; guess unless instructed otherwise
13. Leave time for review

   b. Essay questions
     1. Read each question carefully
     2. Determine exactly what is wanted. Underline key words or phrases.
     3. Decide on outline or paragraph answer
     4. Include many different points and elements unless asked to develop any one or two points or elements
     5. Show impartiality by giving pros and cons unless directed to select one side only
     6. Make and write down any assumptions you find necessary to answer the questions
     7. Watch your English, grammar, punctuation and choice of words
     8. Time your answers; don't crowd material

8) Answering the essay question

Most essay questions can be answered by framing the specific response around several key words or ideas. Here are a few such key words or ideas:

M's: manpower, materials, methods, money, management
P's: purpose, program, policy, plan, procedure, practice, problems, pitfalls, personnel, public relations

   a. Six basic steps in handling problems:
     1. Preliminary plan and background development
     2. Collect information, data and facts
     3. Analyze and interpret information, data and facts
     4. Analyze and develop solutions as well as make recommendations
     5. Prepare report and sell recommendations
     6. Install recommendations and follow up effectiveness

   b. Pitfalls to avoid
     1. *Taking things for granted* – A statement of the situation does not necessarily imply that each of the elements is necessarily true; for example, a complaint may be invalid and biased so that all that can be taken for granted is that a complaint has been registered

2. *Considering only one side of a situation* – Wherever possible, indicate several alternatives and then point out the reasons you selected the best one
3. *Failing to indicate follow up* – Whenever your answer indicates action on your part, make certain that you will take proper follow-up action to see how successful your recommendations, procedures or actions turn out to be
4. *Taking too long in answering any single question* – Remember to time your answers properly

IX. AFTER THE TEST

Scoring procedures differ in detail among civil service jurisdictions although the general principles are the same. Whether the papers are hand-scored or graded by machine we have described, they are nearly always graded by number. That is, the person who marks the paper knows only the number – never the name – of the applicant. Not until all the papers have been graded will they be matched with names. If other tests, such as training and experience or oral interview ratings have been given, scores will be combined. Different parts of the examination usually have different weights. For example, the written test might count 60 percent of the final grade, and a rating of training and experience 40 percent. In many jurisdictions, veterans will have a certain number of points added to their grades.

After the final grade has been determined, the names are placed in grade order and an eligible list is established. There are various methods for resolving ties between those who get the same final grade – probably the most common is to place first the name of the person whose application was received first. Job offers are made from the eligible list in the order the names appear on it. You will be notified of your grade and your rank as soon as all these computations have been made. This will be done as rapidly as possible.

People who are found to meet the requirements in the announcement are called "eligibles." Their names are put on a list of eligible candidates. An eligible's chances of getting a job depend on how high he stands on this list and how fast agencies are filling jobs from the list.

When a job is to be filled from a list of eligibles, the agency asks for the names of people on the list of eligibles for that job. When the civil service commission receives this request, it sends to the agency the names of the three people highest on this list. Or, if the job to be filled has specialized requirements, the office sends the agency the names of the top three persons who meet these requirements from the general list.

The appointing officer makes a choice from among the three people whose names were sent to him. If the selected person accepts the appointment, the names of the others are put back on the list to be considered for future openings.

That is the rule in hiring from all kinds of eligible lists, whether they are for typist, carpenter, chemist, or something else. For every vacancy, the appointing officer has his choice of any one of the top three eligibles on the list. This explains why the person whose name is on top of the list sometimes does not get an appointment when some of the persons lower on the list do. If the appointing officer chooses the second or third eligible, the No. 1 eligible does not get a job at once, but stays on the list until he is appointed or the list is terminated.

X. HOW TO PASS THE INTERVIEW TEST

The examination for which you applied requires an oral interview test. You have already taken the written test and you are now being called for the interview test – the final part of the formal examination.

You may think that it is not possible to prepare for an interview test and that there are no procedures to follow during an interview. Our purpose is to point out some things you can do in advance that will help you and some good rules to follow and pitfalls to avoid while you are being interviewed.

What is an interview supposed to test?

The written examination is designed to test the technical knowledge and competence of the candidate; the oral is designed to evaluate intangible qualities, not readily measured otherwise, and to establish a list showing the relative fitness of each candidate – as measured against his competitors – for the position sought. Scoring is not on the basis of "right" and "wrong," but on a sliding scale of values ranging from "not passable" to "outstanding." As a matter of fact, it is possible to achieve a relatively low score without a single "incorrect" answer because of evident weakness in the qualities being measured.

Occasionally, an examination may consist entirely of an oral test – either an individual or a group oral. In such cases, information is sought concerning the technical knowledges and abilities of the candidate, since there has been no written examination for this purpose. More commonly, however, an oral test is used to supplement a written examination.

Who conducts interviews?

The composition of oral boards varies among different jurisdictions. In nearly all, a representative of the personnel department serves as chairman. One of the members of the board may be a representative of the department in which the candidate would work. In some cases, "outside experts" are used, and, frequently, a businessman or some other representative of the general public is asked to serve. Labor and management or other special groups may be represented. The aim is to secure the services of experts in the appropriate field.

However the board is composed, it is a good idea (and not at all improper or unethical) to ascertain in advance of the interview who the members are and what groups they represent. When you are introduced to them, you will have some idea of their backgrounds and interests, and at least you will not stutter and stammer over their names.

What should be done before the interview?

While knowledge about the board members is useful and takes some of the surprise element out of the interview, there is other preparation which is more substantive. It *is* possible to prepare for an oral interview – in several ways:

1) Keep a copy of your application and review it carefully before the interview

This may be the only document before the oral board, and the starting point of the interview. Know what education and experience you have listed there, and the sequence and dates of all of it. Sometimes the board will ask you to review the highlights of your experience for them; you should not have to hem and haw doing it.

2) Study the class specification and the examination announcement

Usually, the oral board has one or both of these to guide them. The qualities, characteristics or knowledges required by the position sought are stated in these documents. They offer valuable clues as to the nature of the oral interview. For example, if the job involves supervisory responsibilities, the announcement will usually indicate that knowledge of modern supervisory methods and the qualifications of the candidate as a supervisor will be tested. If so, you can expect such questions, frequently in the form of a hypothetical situation which you are expected to solve. NEVER go into an oral without knowledge of the duties and responsibilities of the job you seek.

3) Think through each qualification required

Try to visualize the kind of questions you would ask if you were a board member. How well could you answer them? Try especially to appraise your own knowledge and background in each area, *measured against the job sought*, and identify any areas in which you are weak. Be critical and realistic – do not flatter yourself.

4) Do some general reading in areas in which you feel you may be weak

For example, if the job involves supervision and your past experience has NOT, some general reading in supervisory methods and practices, particularly in the field of human relations, might be useful. Do NOT study agency procedures or detailed manuals. The oral board will be testing your understanding and capacity, not your memory.

5) Get a good night's sleep and watch your general health and mental attitude

You will want a clear head at the interview. Take care of a cold or any other minor ailment, and of course, no hangovers.

What should be done on the day of the interview?

Now comes the day of the interview itself. Give yourself plenty of time to get there. Plan to arrive somewhat ahead of the scheduled time, particularly if your appointment is in the fore part of the day. If a previous candidate fails to appear, the board might be ready for you a bit early. By early afternoon an oral board is almost invariably behind schedule if there are many candidates, and you may have to wait. Take along a book or magazine to read, or your application to review, but leave any extraneous material in the waiting room when you go in for your interview. In any event, relax and compose yourself.

The matter of dress is important. The board is forming impressions about you – from your experience, your manners, your attitude, and your appearance. Give your personal appearance careful attention. Dress your best, but not your flashiest. Choose conservative, appropriate clothing, and be sure it is immaculate. This is a business interview, and your appearance should indicate that you regard it as such. Besides, being well groomed and properly dressed will help boost your confidence.

Sooner or later, someone will call your name and escort you into the interview room. *This is it.* From here on you are on your own. It is too late for any more preparation. But remember, you asked for this opportunity to prove your fitness, and you are here because your request was granted.

What happens when you go in?

The usual sequence of events will be as follows: The clerk (who is often the board stenographer) will introduce you to the chairman of the oral board, who will introduce you to the other members of the board. Acknowledge the introductions before you sit down. Do not be surprised if you find a microphone facing you or a stenotypist sitting by. Oral interviews are usually recorded in the event of an appeal or other review.

Usually the chairman of the board will open the interview by reviewing the highlights of your education and work experience from your application – primarily for the benefit of the other members of the board, as well as to get the material into the record. Do not interrupt or comment unless there is an error or significant misinterpretation; if that is the case, do not hesitate. But do not quibble about insignificant matters. Also, he will usually ask you some question about your education, experience or your present job – partly to get you to start talking and to establish the interviewing "rapport." He may start the actual questioning, or turn it over to one of the other members. Frequently, each member undertakes the questioning on a particular area, one in which he is perhaps most competent, so you can expect each member to participate in the examination. Because time is limited, you may also expect some rather abrupt switches in the direction the questioning takes, so do not be upset by it. Normally, a board member will not pursue a single line of questioning unless he discovers a particular strength or weakness.

After each member has participated, the chairman will usually ask whether any member has any further questions, then will ask you if you have anything you wish to add. Unless you are expecting this question, it may floor you. Worse, it may start you off on an extended, extemporaneous speech. The board is not usually seeking more information. The question is principally to offer you a last opportunity to present further qualifications or to indicate that you have nothing to add. So, if you feel that a significant qualification or characteristic has been overlooked, it is proper to point it out in a sentence or so. Do not compliment the board on the thoroughness of their examination – they have been sketchy, and you know it. If you wish, merely say, "No thank you, I have nothing further to add." This is a point where you can "talk yourself out" of a good impression or fail to present an important bit of information. Remember, *you close the interview yourself*.

The chairman will then say, "That is all, Mr. _____, thank you." Do not be startled; the interview is over, and quicker than you think. Thank him, gather your belongings and take your leave. Save your sigh of relief for the other side of the door.

How to put your best foot forward

Throughout this entire process, you may feel that the board individually and collectively is trying to pierce your defenses, seek out your hidden weaknesses and embarrass and confuse you. Actually, this is not true. They are obliged to make an appraisal of your qualifications for the job you are seeking, and they want to see you in your best light. Remember, they must interview all candidates and a non-cooperative candidate may become a failure in spite of their best efforts to bring out his qualifications. Here are 15 suggestions that will help you:

1) Be natural – Keep your attitude confident, not cocky

If you are not confident that you can do the job, do not expect the board to be. Do not apologize for your weaknesses, try to bring out your strong points. The board is interested in a positive, not negative, presentation. Cockiness will antagonize any board member and make him wonder if you are covering up a weakness by a false show of strength.

2) Get comfortable, but don't lounge or sprawl

Sit erectly but not stiffly. A careless posture may lead the board to conclude that you are careless in other things, or at least that you are not impressed by the importance of the occasion. Either conclusion is natural, even if incorrect. Do not fuss with your clothing, a pencil or an ashtray. Your hands may occasionally be useful to emphasize a point; do not let them become a point of distraction.

3) Do not wisecrack or make small talk

This is a serious situation, and your attitude should show that you consider it as such. Further, the time of the board is limited – they do not want to waste it, and neither should you.

4) Do not exaggerate your experience or abilities
In the first place, from information in the application or other interviews and sources, the board may know more about you than you think. Secondly, you probably will not get away with it. An experienced board is rather adept at spotting such a situation, so do not take the chance.

5) If you know a board member, do not make a point of it, yet do not hide it
Certainly you are not fooling him, and probably not the other members of the board. Do not try to take advantage of your acquaintanceship – it will probably do you little good.

6) Do not dominate the interview
Let the board do that. They will give you the clues – do not assume that you have to do all the talking. Realize that the board has a number of questions to ask you, and do not try to take up all the interview time by showing off your extensive knowledge of the answer to the first one.

7) Be attentive
You only have 20 minutes or so, and you should keep your attention at its sharpest throughout. When a member is addressing a problem or question to you, give him your undivided attention. Address your reply principally to him, but do not exclude the other board members.

8) Do not interrupt
A board member may be stating a problem for you to analyze. He will ask you a question when the time comes. Let him state the problem, and wait for the question.

9) Make sure you understand the question
Do not try to answer until you are sure what the question is. If it is not clear, restate it in your own words or ask the board member to clarify it for you. However, do not haggle about minor elements.

10) Reply promptly but not hastily
A common entry on oral board rating sheets is "candidate responded readily," or "candidate hesitated in replies." Respond as promptly and quickly as you can, but do not jump to a hasty, ill-considered answer.

11) Do not be peremptory in your answers
A brief answer is proper – but do not fire your answer back. That is a losing game from your point of view. The board member can probably ask questions much faster than you can answer them.

12) Do not try to create the answer you think the board member wants
He is interested in what kind of mind you have and how it works – not in playing games. Furthermore, he can usually spot this practice and will actually grade you down on it.

13) Do not switch sides in your reply merely to agree with a board member
Frequently, a member will take a contrary position merely to draw you out and to see if you are willing and able to defend your point of view. Do not start a debate, yet do not surrender a good position. If a position is worth taking, it is worth defending.

14) Do not be afraid to admit an error in judgment if you are shown to be wrong

The board knows that you are forced to reply without any opportunity for careful consideration. Your answer may be demonstrably wrong. If so, admit it and get on with the interview.

15) Do not dwell at length on your present job

The opening question may relate to your present assignment. Answer the question but do not go into an extended discussion. You are being examined for a *new* job, not your present one. As a matter of fact, try to phrase ALL your answers in terms of the job for which you are being examined.

Basis of Rating

Probably you will forget most of these "do's" and "don'ts" when you walk into the oral interview room. Even remembering them all will not ensure you a passing grade. Perhaps you did not have the qualifications in the first place. But remembering them will help you to put your best foot forward, without treading on the toes of the board members.

Rumor and popular opinion to the contrary notwithstanding, an oral board wants you to make the best appearance possible. They know you are under pressure – but they also want to see how you respond to it as a guide to what your reaction would be under the pressures of the job you seek. They will be influenced by the degree of poise you display, the personal traits you show and the manner in which you respond.

ABOUT THIS BOOK

This book contains tests divided into Examination Sections. Go through each test, answering every question in the margin. We have also attached a sample answer sheet at the back of the book that can be removed and used. At the end of each test look at the answer key and check your answers. On the ones you got wrong, look at the right answer choice and learn. Do not fill in the answers first. Do not memorize the questions and answers, but understand the answer and principles involved. On your test, the questions will likely be different from the samples. Questions are changed and new ones added. If you understand these past questions you should have success with any changes that arise. Tests may consist of several types of questions. We have additional books on each subject should more study be advisable or necessary for you. Finally, the more you study, the better prepared you will be. This book is intended to be the last thing you study before you walk into the examination room. Prior study of relevant texts is also recommended. NLC publishes some of these in our Fundamental Series. Knowledge and good sense are important factors in passing your exam. Good luck also helps. So now study this Passbook, absorb the material contained within and take that knowledge into the examination. Then do your best to pass that exam.

EXAMINATION SECTION

EXAMINATION SECTION
TEST 1

DIRECTIONS: Each question or incomplete statement is followed by several suggested answers or completions. Select the one that BEST answers the question or completes the statement. *PRINT THE LETTER OF THE CORRECT ANSWER IN THE SPACE AT THE RIGHT.*

1. The Law position is used to obtain x-rays of the   1.____

    A. jugular foramina   B. mandible
    C. mastoid process   D. petrous portions

2. Assume that the roentgenologist has requested a ventral decubitus view of the lungs. The technician adjusts the patient's body to a true anteroposterior position with the arms above the head. He places the cassette vertically against the affected side. The exposure is then made at the end of a full inhalation.   2.____
    In reviewing the procedure described above, it would be CORRECT to say that the

    A. body should have been in a true posteroanterior position
    B. patient should have been in an erect position
    C. exposure should have been made on expiration
    D. technician followed the correct procedure

3. If a fracture of the lateral malleolus is suspected, the films which should be taken are   3.____

    A. AP and lateral views of the knee
    B. AP, lateral, and oblique views of the ankle
    C. AP, lateral, and oblique views of the elbow
    D. skull, submentovertex view

4. For an infusion nephropyelography, it is necessary to use a table that is equipped with   4.____

    A. a cystoscopy unit   B. cine radiography
    C. enema apparatus   D. tomographic apparatus

5. In pneumoencephalography, the area which is studied is the   5.____

    A. heart
    B. lungs
    C. spinal cord
    D. ventricular system of the brain

6. In order to determine fluid level in the chest, the position which should be used, in addition to routine views, is   6.____

    A. AP decubitus   B. LAO and RAO
    C. lateral decubitus   D. PA decubitus

7. The position for the cervical spine which should be used to obtain views of the atlas and axis is   7.____

    A. AP, open mouth   B. LAO
    C. lateral   D. RAO

8. The palpation points for a lateral position of the sternum are the

   A. acromion process and the xyphoid process
   B. apex of the scapula and the manubrium
   C. manubrium and the xyphoid process
   D. sterno-clavicular articulation and the shaft of the clavicle

9. The one of the following procedures which does NOT require the use of a contrast medium is

   A. cerebral angiography
   B. cholangiography
   C. myelography
   D. xeroradiography

10. In order to secure a radiograph of the pars petrosapro-jected at right angles to its long axis, one should use

    A. Fuch's position
    B. Hickey's position
    C. Stenver's position
    D. the anterior tangential view

11. In an I.V.P. examination of the average adult patient, the compensation for the kidney drop when the patient is moved from the supine to the erect position is approximately _____ inches.

    A. twelve   B. six   C. two   D. zero

12. The Chassard-Lapine position is used to demonstrate the

    A. cervical spine
    B. hip joint
    C. pelvis
    D. sigmoid

13. The lordotic projection of the chest is used MAINLY to demonstrate the

    A. apices
    B. diaphragm
    C. great vessels
    D. size of the heart

14. In the Granger position for an x-ray of the sella turcica, the central ray is directed

    A. 10° caudad
    B. 10° cephalad
    C. 30° cephalad
    D. perpendicularly

15. In a radiograph of the kidneys, the left kidney when compared with the right kidney is USUALLY

    A. much larger
    B. on the same level
    C. slightly higher
    D. slightly lower

16. Of the following, the one which is a measurement of x-ray quantity is

    A. a milliampere
    B. a roentgen
    C. an angstrom
    D. the half-value layer

17. The quality of an x-ray beam is MAINLY dependent on the

    A. heat of the filament
    B. KvP impressed on the tube
    C. size of the focal spot
    D. size of the target

18. The *half-value layer* is the measure which has been adopted internationally to indicate   18.____

    A. radiation quality
    B. radiation quantity
    C. the amount of filtration to be added in x-ray therapy
    D. the inherent filtration in an x-ray tube

19. An increase in the kilovoltage across the x-ray tube results in   19.____

    A. no alteration in wave length
    B. radiation of longer wave length
    C. radiation of shorter wave length
    D. twice as many impulses per second

20. The CHIEF purpose of a filter of aluminum placed beneath the aperture of a radiographic tube is to   20.____

    A. control the latitude of the radiographic image
    B. eliminate the light given off by the filament
    C. absorb some of the longer wave lengths
    D. filter out undesirable stem radiation

21. The autotransformer is used to   21.____

    A. dissipate the heat in the x-ray tube
    B. measure the time of exposure
    C. select the milliamperes to be used
    D. select the voltage to the high tension transformer

22. The ratio of a transformer expresses the relationship of   22.____

    A. the number of turns in the primary winding to the number of turns in the secondary winding
    B. the weight of the primary to the weight of the secondary
    C. the size of the wire in the primary to the size of the wire in the secondary
    D. watts output to watts input

23. The milliamperage through the x-ray tube for any given exposure is CHIEFLY dependent upon the   23.____

    A. heat of the anode
    B. heat of the filament
    C. size of the target
    D. voltage applied to the tube

24. A rheostat changes the voltage by   24.____

    A. cutting out part of the transformer
    B. increasing the number of windings in the primary of the transformer
    C. shortening the filament transformer
    D. varying the amount of resistance

25. If an x-ray tube is gassy, it will USUALLY be noted that

    A. no reading will be obtained on the primary voltmeter
    B. the milliammeter is not registering
    C. there are irregular fluctuations in the milliamperage
    D. the tube filament does not light up

26. The ADVANTAGE of a rotating anode x-ray tube over stationary anode tube is that the rotating anode tube

    A. is low in cost
    B. permits lower energies to be used
    C. is small and easily manipulated
    D. permits high energies with a small focal spot

27. During a 100 Ma exposure with full-wave rectified equipment, a milliammeter which is known to be accurate indicates only 50 Ma.
    Of the following, the MOST probable reason for this is that

    A. a valve tube is not functioning properly
    B. one of the fuses is burned out
    C. the high tension transformer has developed a short circuit
    D. the timer is not properly set

28. A double focus x-ray tube is one which has

    A. two cathodes
    B. two electrodes
    C. two focal spots
    D. rotating and stationary anodes

29. A spinning top is used to check the timer of a full-wave rectified x-ray machine.
    If an exposure is made at 1/10 of a second, and the timer is accurate, the number of black dots which will show on the processed film is

    A. 6   B. 8   C. 10   D. 12

30. In a full-wave rectified x-ray unit, if one of the valve-tubes is nonfunctioning, the milliammeter will register

    A. double the selected Ma
    B. slightly more than one-half of the selected Ma
    C. the same as the selected Ma
    D. zero

31. High speed screens are NOT ordinarily useful in

    A. intravenous urography
    B. magnification radiography
    C. pediatric radiography
    D. radiography of the hand

32. Of the following, the MOST important reason for keeping records in an x-ray department is to provide

A. a basis for evaluating the performance of the individual employees in the department
B. an easy way to predict the next year's work load
C. better health care to the patients and families in the community
D. statistical information for reporting on the activities of the x-ray department

33. The one of the following which it is LEAST necessary for the technician to record on every x-ray film is the

   A. date of examination
   B. name of the doctor
   C. name of the patient
   D. side (R or L)

34. The MOST important reason for paying attention to a complaint from a patient who has come for an examination is that

   A. people appreciate the attention given to their complaints
   B. employees should always be considerate to patients
   C. there is no harm in listening, even if the complaint is not justified
   D. there may be good reason for the patient's complaint

35. To gain the confidence of the patient, it would be MOST advisable for the technician to

   A. discuss the patient's symptoms with the patient
   B. let the patient know he is friendly with the physicians
   C. present an efficient and careful manner of work
   D. tell the patient about his training and experience as a technician

36. Assume that one of the two x-ray rooms is unavailable for use on a day when a large number of patients have been scheduled for examination.
    Of the following, it would be BEST to

   A. proceed with the examination of all patients, taking them in order as scheduled
   B. reschedule all of the afternoon patients since it will be impossible to reach them before closing time
   C. see if any of the patients can come on another date and arrange for appointments at the next suitable date for these patients
   D. take only half of the patients called for each hour, and tell the others to come back on another date

37. An elderly woman who is scheduled for a series of radio-grans tells the technician halfway through the session that she feels nauseous and does not want to continue.
    Of the following, it would be BEST for the technician to

   A. ask her if she can come back the next day since it is important that the series be completed
   B. ask her if she would like to rest outside while he takes another patient, and say that he will continue her examination when she feels better
   C. tell her he has not completed the series but that, if she chooses to stop, it is her responsibility
   D. tell her that she will have to continue until the full series is completed

38. For a technician to discuss the x-ray findings with the patient's family would be   38.____
    A. *wise,* because the family would be favorably impressed with the technician's knowledge and ability
    B. *unwise,* because the family should be told by the radiologist or doctor in charge of the case of the diagnosis and treatment required
    C. *wise,* because he would be able to assure them that the patient's condition is not serious since he has seen the films
    D. *unwise,* because the technician is too busy to be able to enter into discussion of the patient's condition with the family

39. The radiologist who is in charge of the section frequently, and without prior announcement, gives the technicians assignments in the department which conflict with those of their immediate supervisor.   39.____
    In order to resolve the conflict, it would be BEST for the
    A. supervisor to discuss the matter with the radiologist at some convenient time
    B. technicians to discuss the matter with the radiologist while the supervisor is present
    C. supervisor to tell the technicians to follow the radiologist's orders
    D. supervisor to tell the technicians to ignore the radiologist and do the work he has assigned

40. One of the technicians is trying hard to do a good job but seems to lack the needed skills for good work.   40.____
    In this situation, it would be BEST for the supervisor to
    A. arrange to give this technician additional training
    B. assign less difficult work to this technician
    C. let the technician learn by doing
    D. set lower performance standards for this technician

KEY (CORRECT ANSWERS)

1.	C	11.	C	21.	D	31.	D
2.	A	12.	D	22.	A	32.	C
3.	B	13.	A	23.	B	33.	B
4.	D	14.	B	24.	D	34.	D
5.	D	15.	C	25.	C	35.	C
6.	C	16.	B	26.	D	36.	C
7.	A	17.	B	27.	A	37.	B
8.	C	18.	A	28.	C	38.	B
9.	D	19.	C	29.	D	39.	A
10.	C	20.	C	30.	B	40.	A

TEST 2

DIRECTIONS: Each question or incomplete statement is followed by several suggested answers or completions. Select the one that BEST answers the question or completes the statement. *PRINT THE LETTER OF THE CORRECT ANSWER IN THE SPACE AT THE RIGHT.*

1. The primary purpose of filters in a film badge used for x-ray detection is to

   A. absorb scattered radiation
   B. increase the gamma of the H and D curve
   C. permit dose measurements over a wide range of energies
   D. prevent fogging

   1.____

2. Of the following, the statement about grids which is NOT correct is:

   A. Focused grids should be used only within fixed target-film distance ranges
   B. Grids reduce the scattered radiation that reaches the film
   C. Simple grids limit the size of the radiograph
   D. To prevent grid shadows, the grid and tube are moved separately

   2.____

3. Of the following, the statement about screens which is NOT correct is:

   A. Generally, faster screens give poorer resolution
   B. Screens give better resolution
   C. Screens reduce the x-ray exposure of the film
   D. Screens should be used only with screen film

   3.____

4. A Potter-Bucky diaphragm is used CHIEFLY to

   A. eliminate a large percentage of secondary radiation
   B. increase the diameter of the primary beam
   C. limit the diameter of the primary beam
   D. produce radiographs free from distortion

   4.____

5. A crosshatched grid is NOT useful

   A. at a 20° angle into the grid
   B. at 60 inch anode-film distance
   C. in pediatric radiology
   D. with off-center perpendicular beam techniques

   5.____

6. Sharpness of detail on a diagnostic radiograph is NOT ordinarily affected by

   A. grid ratio
   B. movement of the patient
   C. screen speed
   D. target size

   6.____

7. In fluoroscopy, reducing the size of the field results in an improved image because of less scatter from the

   A. collimator shutters
   B. table top
   C. patient
   D. room

   7.____

8. A film is taken with a target-film distance of 40 inches and an object-film distance of 10 inches.
   The magnification factor is

   A. .45   B. .60   C. 1.20   D. 1.33

9. In half-wave rectified x-ray machines operating with a 60 cycle current, the number of impulses per second passing through the tube is

   A. 20   B. 40   C. 50   D. 60

10. An x-ray tube with a heat-storage capacity of 100,000 heat units has a cooling rate of 10,000 heat units per minute. Starting with a cold tube, a certain procedure calls for 5 exposures of 100 Kv, 500 Ma and 1/5 second each. After 3 minutes, a second series of 10 films is to be taken.
    Which of the following techniques would NOT damage this tube?
    _____ Kv, _____ Ma, _____ second(s).

    A. 80; 100; 2   B. 80; 500; 1/5
    C. 100; 500; 1/5   D. 120; 300; 1/3

11. All other factors being equal, which of the following exposures would produce the greatest radiographic density?
    _____ second and _____ milliamperes.

    A. 1/10; 100   B. 1/20; 200   C. 1/40; 500   D. 1; 10

12. Fine focus (0.3 mm.) anode tubes

    A. allow direct magnification radiography
    B. are not desirable for vascular radiology
    C. cannot be used with rotating anodes
    D. require three phase input

13. In an image-amplifier fluoroscopic system with automatic brightness control, moving to a thicker part of the patient AUTOMATICALLY

    A. decreases the Kv to give more contrast
    B. increases the brightness setting on the TV monitor
    C. increases the gain of the image-amplifier tube
    D. increases the Kv or Ma of the x-ray tube

14. Three phase x-ray units

    A. allow shorter exposure times
    B. are not useful in serial rapid film techniques
    C. increase contrast at the same Kv settings as in single phase units
    D. require higher Kv settings

15. The thickness of cut in linear tomography depends on the

    A. anatomy of the patient   B. Kv used
    C. length of sweep   D. Ma used

16. The one of the following which is NOT a function of a radiographic cone is to

    A. decrease contrast
    B. decrease secondary scatter
    C. improve detail visibility
    D. limit the field of exposure

17. If all other factors are kept constant, the change from a two mm to a one mm focal spot will produce a radiograph with

    A. increased distortion
    B. magnification
    C. poorer definition
    D. sharper image

18. If all other factors are kept constant, the change from non-grid to grid technique will produce a radiograph with

    A. decreased contrast
    B. increased contrast
    C. increased density
    D. no change in contrast or density

19. The optimum distance between the x-ray tube and the grid is determined by the

    A. distance between lead strips
    B. grid ratio
    C. height of lead strips
    D. number of lead strips

20. Suppose that a film has been taken with Kv of 60. A second film, taken at Kv of 70, with all other factors unchanged, would show ALMOST_____ the exposure.

    A. one-seventh
    B. one-sixth
    C. one-half
    D. twice

21. Assume that for a particular radiograph which is normally taken at 72 inch distance and 10 MaS, it is necessary to reduce the distance to 36 inches.
    The new MaS should be

    A. 2.5   B. 5   C. 10   D. 20

22. To reduce patient exposure to radiation, the x-ray beam should be filtered by the equivalent of

    A. 3 cm of aluminum
    B. 3 mm of aluminum
    C. 3 mm of coppor
    D. 3 mm of tungsten

23. The maximum permissible milliamperage during fluoroscopy is

    A. 1   B. 3   C. 5   D. 7

24. The maximum permissible dose in rads to the whole body for a radiation worker who is 30 years old is

    A. 30   B. 60   C. 90   D. 120

25. The radiation dose to a technician should not exceed

    A. 3 rem in 13 weeks B. 3 rem in 1 year
    C. 15 rem in 1 year   D. 30 rem in 1 month

26. Reversal of the radiographic image is produced by

    A. chemical fog
    B. exposure of film to white light
    C. film touching the sides of the tank
    D. overexposure of film to radiation

27. The yellowing of processed radiographs after they have been stored for a period of time is the result of

    A. inadequate developing
    B. inadequate rinsing after developing
    C. inadequate washing
    D. weak developer

28. The suspended crystals embedded in the gelatin of the x-ray film are

    A. calcium tungstate B. silver bromide
    C. silver nitrate   D. zinc sulfide

29. Film artifacts appearing as branching, twig-like lines are caused by

    A. fingernail scratches
    B. improper processing
    C. improper safelight exposure
    D. static

30. Elon and hydroquinone in the developer acts as

    A. acidifiers   B. developing agents
    C. preservatives   D. restrainers

31. If a patient must be held during radiography, the person who holds the patient should be

    A. a technician who is most familiar with the position used
    B. anyone who is available at the time
    C. one who is not regularly exposed to radiation
    D. the technician who has had the lowest radiation exposure in the past six months

32. Compared to a 14 x 17 PA chest film exposure, a miniature chest photofluorogram will

    A. be equally satisfactory for diagnostic purposes
    B. give better definition for diagnostic purposes
    C. result in a higher radiation dose to the patient
    D. result in a lower radiation dose to the patient

33. A patient presents the technician with a note signed by his doctor, requesting that he be allowed to borrow films of his gall bladder series in order for a comparison to be made with an earlier series.
    Of the following, it would be BEST for the technician to

A. give him the films but keep the doctor's note
B. give him the films since they are his
C. obtain the permission of the radiologist to give him the films
D. inform him that the films cannot be borrowed

34. You have instructed an aide who is responsible for the supply room to use those supplies which have been on hand longest before using newer stock.
Of the following, the MOST practical way to do this is to

    A. keep a file for each item in supply, with records of dates when supplies are received and used
    B. place new supplies behind those of different items which are already in stock
    C. put newly-received supplies in the supply closet only after all supplies of the same item are used up
    D. put supplies that are needed most often in the front of the supply closet

35. Assume that, because of alterations in the building, the x-ray department in the health center is being redesigned and you have been asked to make suggestions.
Before planning the new layout, it would be MOST important to know

    A. how many employees will be assigned to the x-ray department
    B. how much money will be available for the alterations in the x-ray department
    C. the probable location of the x-ray department in the building
    D. what types and numbers of x-ray examinations will be required of this department

36. Suppose a meeting of the technicians has been called to discuss ways of improving certain procedures and practices in the x-ray departments at the various locations.
Of the following, the LEAST desirable result of the meeting would be

    A. the adjustment of differences in point of view within the group
    B. the demonstration of the supervisor's ability to lead rather than control the group by command
    C. the motivation of the members of the group to work in harmony
    D. to show the group that the supervisor's ideas are always correct

37. Suppose the services of part-time aides have been made available. These aides will be assigned, as needed, to work in the x-ray departments of the various health centers. One of the technicians objects to working with these aides.
Of the following, the action which would be MOST appropriate for the supervisor to take to change this technician's attitude would be to

    A. agree with him that part-time aides will not be very useful, but explain to him that he cannot refuse to use them
    B. discuss with him some of the ways that aides might be useful in the x-ray department
    C. explain to him that these part-time aides need and are entitled to work experience
    D. tell him that use of part-time aides may result in large raises for the technicians because of increased work output

38. Assume that you are attending a training session for a group of x-ray technicians.
Of the following, the LEAST important reason for asking questions during the session is to

A. check on the effectiveness of the teaching
B. find out who is the best technician in the group
C. focus attention on an important point in the lesson
D. motivate the group to pay attention to the lecture

39. In the orientation training of a newly-appointed technician, it would be LEAST helpful to

    A. discuss the importance of careful positioning of patients in x-ray examination
    B. point out the charts used in determining exposure factors for the available equipment
    C. review the anatomical terms commonly used in radiography
    D. stress the clinical importance of accurate radiography in the treatment of patients

40. Assume that you are teaching a less experienced technician the correct way to take one of the more complicated radiographs.
    Of the following, the BEST procedure to follow is to

    A. explain what is to be done; then demonstrate how it is done; then observe him as he does it himself, making corrections if needed; then follow up
    B. prepare a detailed, step-by-step explanation in writing for the technician to follow, and tell him to speak to you if he has any questions
    C. show him how to do the easier steps first; then, after he has had some experience, show him the more difficult steps
    D. tell him to watch another, more experienced technician as he performs this task, and to consult with this employee if he has any problems when he has to do it himself

KEY (CORRECT ANSWERS)

1. C	11. C	21. A	31. C
2. C	12. A	22. D	32. C
3. B	13. D	23. C	33. C
4. A	14. A	24. B	34. A
5. A	15. C	25. A	35. D
6. A	16. A	26. B	36. D
7. C	17. D	27. C	37. B
8. D	18. B	28. B	38. B
9. D	19. B	29. D	39. C
10. B	20. D	30. B	40. A

TEST 3

DIRECTIONS: Each question or incomplete statement is followed by several suggested answers or completions. Select the one that BEST answers the question or completes the statement. *PRINT THE LETTER OF ThE CORRECT ANSWER IN THE SPACE AT THE RIGHT.*

1. Vessels which convey blood away from the heart are called   1.____

   A. arteries
   B. lymphatics
   C. veins
   D. ventricles

2. The cardiac orifice is the opening between the   2.____

   A. bronchus and trachea
   B. esophagus and stomach
   C. left ventricle and aorta
   D. superior vena cava and left atrium

3. The double-walled serous membrane enclosing each lung is called the   3.____

   A. pericardium
   B. pleura
   C. meninges
   D. omentum

4. The muscle of the heart is called the   4.____

   A. endocardium
   B. mesocardium
   C. myocardium
   D. pericardium

5. After urine is formed in the kidney, the structures through which it passes until it is voided are, *in order,* the   5.____

   A. bladder, ureter, urethra
   B. ureter, bladder, uvula
   C. ureter, bladder, urethra
   D. urethra, bladder, ureter

6. A sac-like bulging or ballooning of the wall of a blood vessel is known as   6.____

   A. a diverticulum
   B. an aneurysm
   C. a thrombus
   D. phlebitis

7. The collapse of the lung or any portion of it is called   7.____

   A. atelectasis
   B. emphysema
   C. infarct
   D. pneumonitis

8. The angle formed by the lungs and the diaphragm at the lateral chest wall is called the _____ angle.   8.____

   A. costal
   B. costophrenic
   C. intercostal
   D. phrenic

9. The condition in which there is air in the pleural cavity is   9.____

   A. atelectasis
   B. bronchiectasis
   C. empyema
   D. pneumothorax

10. The Islets of Langerhans are ductless glands located in the

    A. kidneys
    B. pancreas
    C. small intestine
    D. spleen

11. The appendix is attached to the

    A. cecum
    B. descending colon
    C. ileum
    D. transverse colon

12. The common bile duct empties into the

    A. duodenum
    B. gall bladder
    C. liver
    D. stomach

13. The ribs that articulate with the sternum are

    A. costochondrals
    B. false ribs
    C. floating ribs
    D. true ribs

14. The organ which lies posterior to the stomach and whose head fits into the duodenal loop is the

    A. gall bladder
    B. kidney
    C. pancreas
    D. pylorus

15. The space between the lungs is called the

    A. ilium
    B. mediastinum
    C. thoracic cavity
    D. thoracic inlet

16. The S-shaped portion of the descending colon is called the

    A. anal canal
    B. ileo-cecal valve
    C. rectum
    D. sigmoid

17. The outer portion of the kidney is the

    A. cortex
    B. hilum
    C. medulla
    D. renal pelvis

18. The head of the femur articulates with the innominate bone to form the hip joint. The cavity in the innominate bone into which the femur fits is the

    A. acetabulum
    B. femoral neck
    C. glenoid fossa
    D. sacro-iliac joint

19. The large opening at the base of the skull through which the spinal cord passes is the

    A. external auditory meatus
    B. foramen magnum
    C. olfactory foramen
    D. optic foramen

20. The three MAJOR divisions of the small intestine, beginning at its upper *end,* are the

    A. duodenum, jejunum, and ileum
    B. duodenum, jejunum, and ischium
    C. ileum, duodenum, and jejunum
    D. jejunum, duodenum, and ileum

21. Striated muscles would be found in the

    A. intima or muscle walls of blood vessels
    B. pituitary gland
    C. biceps
    D. stomach

22. The receptors that are stimulated when the head is rested on the table in front of the chair are in the

    A. temporal lobe   B. semicircular canals
    C. utricle   D. middle ear

23. The neuron that transmits the impulse from the receptor to the spinal cord is the

    A. associative neuron   B. afferent neuron
    C. efferent neuron   D. synaptic connection

24. Those organs or mechanisms that register the movements and position of the body are called

    A. proprioceptors   B. interoceptors
    C. exteroceptors   D. glands

25. The one of the following that does not belong with the others is

    A. axon   B. dendrite   C. end brush   D. pons

26. The MAIN path of communication from higher to lower coordination centers is the

    A. spinal lemniscus   B. pyramidal tracts
    C. pons Varoli   D. medial lemniscus

27. The LARGEST interlobular fissure of the brain is the

    A. fissure of Rolando
    B. parietal-occipital fissure
    C. fissure of Sylvius
    D. longitudinal fissure

28. The pathway the nerve impulse will take through the nervous system is determined by

    A. the length of the central axis from where the impulse enters
    B. the thalamus
    C. synaptic resistance
    D. the cerebellum

29. The four language centers (speaking, writing, hearing, reading) are found in

    A. the cerebellum
    B. both hemispheres of the cerebrum
    C. the spinal cord
    D. the frontal lobe

30. The *motor area* is located in the

    A. cuneas
    B. ascending parietal convolution
    C. superior temporal convolution
    D. precentral gyrus

31. The white matter of the nervous system is due to the

    A. function of conduction   B. synapses present
    C. medullary sheaths   D. structure of nerve cell

32. The one of the following that is NOT related to the other three is

    A. iris   B. pupil   C. retina   D. cochlea

33. The region in the retina in which the vision is clearest is called the

    A. vitreous humor   B. fovea
    C. rod   D. lens

34. The semicircular canals are concerned with

    A. balance   B. muscle sense
    C. hearing   D. pain sensitivity

35. The part of the brain which acts as a relay station for all afferent tracts (except the olfactory and vestibular) and passes these sensory impulses on to the cerebrum is the

    A. medulla   B. precentral gyrus
    C. thalamus   D. cuneas

36. The middle ear consists of the

    A. ossicular chain, the tensor tympani, and the stapedius
    B. tympanic membrance, the malleus, the incus, and the stapes
    C. oval window, the malleus, the incus, and the stapes
    D. Eustachian tube, the malleus, the incus, and the stapes

37. Of the following parts of the larynx, the one which is NOT a cartilage is the

    A. cricoid   B. thyroid
    C. glottis   D. epiglottis

38. Of the following nerves, the one which is NOT concerned with breathing is_____ nerve.

    A. a branch of the 12th thoracic
    B. the phrenic
    C. the vagus
    D. a branch of the 2nd cervical

39. Of the following activities of the body, the one which is NOT under the control of the central nervous system is

    A. digestion   B. breathing
    C. movements of the jaw   D. movements of the tongue

40. Of the following, the one which does NOT involve the use of the cerebrum is 40._____

    A. the sensation of light
    B. the reflex blinking of the eye
    C. the sensation of color awareness
    D. speaking

KEY (CORRECT ANSWERS)

1. A	11. A	21. C	31. C
2. B	12. A	22. C	32. D
3. B	13. D	23. B	33. B
4. C	14. C	24. A	34. A
5. C	15. B	25. D	35. C
6. B	16. D	26. B	36. A
7. A	17. A	27. C	37. C
8. B	18. A	28. C	38. C
9. D	19. B	29. B	39. A
10. B	20. A	30. D	40. B

EXAMINATION SECTION
TEST 1

DIRECTIONS: Each question or incomplete statement is followed by several suggested answers or completions. Select the one that BEST answers the question or completes the statement. *PRINT THE LETTER OF THE CORRECT ANSWER IN THE SPACE AT THE RIGHT.*

1. X-rays were discovered by

    A. Coolidge B. Edison C. Marconi D. Roentgen

2. The *most desirable* end-result of x-ray examination is

    A. proper use of equipment
    B. sufficient number of films
    C. adequate diagnosis
    D. a complete hospital record

3. *Generally*, an x-ray technician should gain the patient's confidence by

    A. an analysis of the patient's case
    B. indicating the type and length of his service in other hospitals
    C. an efficient and thorough manner
    D. friendship with many physicians

4. If a patient asks the x-ray technician a technical diagnostic question dealing with the patient's case, the x-ray technician *should*

    A. answer the question to the best of his ability
    B. refer him to the physician or surgeon
    C. tell the patient to ask again after the films are developed
    D. mention the title of the proper medical textbook dealing with the case

5. An x-ray technician knows that a program to protect himself against the harmful effects of radiation would employ each of the following EXCEPT

    A. sunlight
    B. frequent x-ray examinations
    C. available protective devices
    D. frequent blood counts

6. An ambulatory patient is one who

    A. comes in an ambulance
    B. can walk
    C. is confined to bed
    D. cannot walk, but may come to x-ray in a chair

7. An artefact is a(n)

    A. bone specialist
    B. experienced technician
    C. film defect
    D. film taken at a kilovoltage of over 200 KVP

8. A cervical spine is

   A. part of the neck
   B. part of the pelvis
   C. a projection on the top of an autotransformer
   D. any bony prominence

9. In roentgenology, a filter is used to

   A. lower kilovoltage
   B. lower milliamperage
   C. reduce soft radiation
   D. reduce the emulsion

10. A cathode is a part of the

    A. voltmeter
    B. cable
    C. condenser
    D. x-ray tube

11. An x-ray tube has

    A. air at atmospheric pressure
    B. an almost complete vacuum
    C. neon
    D. freon

12. A sphere gap can be used to measure

    A. kilovoltage
    B. amperage
    C. resistance
    D. impedance

13. A solenoid is a form of

    A. high-tension rectifier
    B. timer
    C. voltmeter
    D. coil magnet

14. A thermostat is a device

    A. attached to a tilt table
    B. employed in radium treatments
    C. used in controlling temperature
    D. for calibrating an x-ray machine

15. A photo-electric cell may be a component part of a(n)

    A. interval timer
    B. rectifying tube circuit
    C. photoroentgen apparatus
    D. kenetron

16. A photoroentgen unit

    A. employs a camera
    B. does tomography
    C. does planigraphy
    D. produces standard density radiographs

17. Tube targets are made of

    A. iron B. uranium
    C. tungsten D. beryllium

18. For protective reasons, some x-ray tubes are housed in a bath of

    A. mercury B. oil
    C. graphite D. tellurium

19. The *usual* contrast material used in a gastro-intestinal series is

    A. bismuth B. barium
    C. bromine D. borax

20. A substance *commonly* used in bronchography is

    A. pantopaque B. priodax
    C. lipiodol D. skiodan

21. A chemical *commonly* used in intensifying screens is

    A. calcium oxalate B. calcium thiocyanate
    C. calcium tungstate D. calcium bicarbonate

22. Filters are used in the x-ray beam to

    A. increase contrast
    B. reduce film density
    C. remove low energy x-ray photon
    D. reduce exposure time

23. X-ray tables should be grounded to **prevent**

    A. motion B. shocks
    C. secondary radiation D. fire hazard

24. A milliampere represents one _____ of an ampere.

    A. *millionth* B. *thousandth*
    C. *hundredth* D. *tenth*

25. The resistance of a conductor to the flow of an electric current is measured by

    A. amperes B. ohms
    C. volts D. watts

26. A rotating anode tube is of value because

    A. a smaller effective focal spot can be used than on ordinary tubes
    B. the rotation of the filament keeps it centered
    C. the rotating anode makes it unnecessary to have a vacuum x-ray tube
    D. a rotating anode makes rectification of current unnecessary

27. On a rotating anode tube, the *average* effective size of the smallest focal spot is *about* _____ sq. mm.

    A. 1 to 2 B. 4 to 8
    C. 16 to 32 D. 50 to 100

28. If the exposure factors are correct for a certain film at 36 inches tube to film distance, and you keep all other factors constant, a film at 6 feet distance will require _____ the time.

    A. one-quarter B. one-half
    C. twice D. four times

29. Compared with intensifying screens, cardboard holders require *about* _____ times as much exposure time.

    A. two B. eight
    C. sixteen D. thirty-two

30. Intensifying screens are used *primarily to*

    A. obtain better detail
    B. obtain better contrast
    C. reduce x-ray energy
    D. shorten target-skin distance

31. Fluoroscopes are *usually* set at about _____ milliamperes.

    A. 5 B. 10 C. 20 D. 40

32. Shock-proof equipment indicates *primarily*

    A. protection from secondary radiation
    B. resistance to rough handling
    C. protection from high tension current
    D. resistance to the pulsation effect in current

33. Technique charts should be used for each of the following reasons EXCEPT to

    A. shorten exposure time B. prevent tube overload
    C. reduce film wastage D. reduce technical error

34. Chest films are *customarily* taken at 6 feet to

    A. protect patient B. reduce motion effect
    C. decrease distortion D. remove artefacts

35. The *minimum* distance of acceptable safety between patient and fluoroscopy tube is _____ inches.

    A. 5 B. 10 C. 20 D. 25

36. Films of the chest for lung detail are *usually* taken on

    A. inspiration B. expiration
    C. phonation D. deglutition

37. When a patient is directly facing the cassette, the position is

    A. A.P B. P.A
    C. supine D. lateral

38. The *opposite* to pronation is

    A. flexion B. extension
    C. lordosis D. supination

39. To demonstrate fluid levels in the chest or abdomen, the x-ray beam **should be**

    A. converging
    B. of low kilovoltage
    C. vertical
    D. horizontal

40. Planigraphy is

    A. soft tissue technique
    B. stereoscopic study
    C. sectional radiography
    D. myelography

41. By "prone" is meant

    A. face down
    B. flat on back
    C. lying on side
    D. semi-recumbent

42. A tangential view means, most nearly, one that is

    A. ordered by radiologist
    B. ordered by head technician
    C. far oblique
    D. taken across a visible mass

43. A bronchogram consists of

    A. stereoscopic chest studies
    B. P.A. and lateral chest
    C. films showing visualization of bronchi with lipiodol
    D. planigraphy

44. An examination of the ilium for fracture involves the

    A. skull
    B. leg
    C. pelvis
    D. foot

45. The knee cap is known technically as the

    A. fabella
    B. patella
    C. os calcis
    D. calvarium

46. The exit of the stomach is called the

    A. cardia
    B. antrum
    C. lesser ourvature
    D. pylorus

47. The urethra is the

    A. inlet to the bladder
    B. outlet of the bladder
    C. upper part of the kidney
    D. lower part of the kidney

48. The *longest* bone in the body is called the

    A. femur
    B. humerus
    C. radius
    D. tibia

49. The pancreatic and bile ducts enter into the

    A. esophagus
    B. stomach
    C. duodenum
    D. colon

50. The opening in the base of the skull where the spinal cord enters is called foramen

    A. of Morgagni
    B. magnum
    C. rotundum
    D. ovale

KEY (CORRECT ANSWERS)

1.	D	11.	B	21.	C	31.	A	41.	A
2.	C	12.	A	22.	C	32.	C	42.	D
3.	C	13.	D	23.	B	33.	A	43.	C
4.	B	14.	C	24.	B	34.	C	44.	C
5.	B	15.	C	25.	B	35.	B	45.	B
6.	B	16.	A	26.	A	36.	A	46.	D
7.	C	17.	C	27.	A	37.	B	47.	B
8.	A	18.	B	28.	D	38.	D	48.	A
9.	C	19.	B	29.	B	39.	D	49.	C
10.	D	20.	C	30.	C	40.	C	50.	B

EXAMINATION SECTION
TEST 1

DIRECTIONS: Each question or incomplete statement is followed by several suggested answers or completions. Select the one that BEST answers the question or completes the statement. *PRINT THE LETTER OF THE CORRECT ANSWER IN THE SPACE AT THE RIGHT.*

1. The symphysis pubis is part of the
   A. pelvis   B. jaw   C. thorax   D. foot

   1._____

2. The sella turcia is in the
   A. center of the base of the skull   B. vertex of the skull
   C. occipital region   D. frontal region

   2._____

3. Stenver's position is used in examination of the
   A. innominate bone   B. os calcis
   C. navicular   D. temporal bone or petrous pyramid

   3._____

4. A tarsal bone is a small bone in the
   A. skull   B. wrist   C. foot   D. pelvis

   4._____

5. In the parotid region, one might look for a _____ calculus.
   A. biliary   B. urinary   C. prostatic   D. salivary

   5._____

6. It is important to have media numbered MAINLY to
   A. prevent loss
   B. replace missing media
   C. locate defective screens and artifacts
   D. keep a good property inventory

   6._____

7. It is important to identify films, but this will NOT lead to
   A. the radiologist knowing left and right
   B. keeping accurate records
   C. hastening film taking
   D. avoiding mixups

   7._____

8. You have obtained a film of proper density of a spine on a 14 x 17 film. You are asked to get a film of one vertebra using a small cone. The exposure factors will be _____ for a 14 x 17 cone.
   A. half as much as   B. slightly less than
   C. slightly greater than   D. twice as much as

   8._____

9. Static marks on films are MOST likely to occur in _____ weather.
   A. hot dry   B. cold dry   C. hot wet   D. cold wet

   9._____

25

10. The ingredient that forms the bulk of the emulsion coating an x-ray film is   10._____
    A. silver bromide   B. iodine   C. gelatin   D. zinc sulphate

11. When a short stop bath is used, the PRINCIPAL ingredient is   11._____
    A. nitric acid   B. sodium hydroxide
    C. elbon   D. acetic acid

12. Normal temperature of a developing solution is _____ degrees F.   12._____
    A. 58 to 60   B. 68 to 70   C. 78 to 80   D. 88 to 90

13. A stop bath is used to   13._____
    A. prevent further developing
    B. retard fixing
    C. give greater detail
    D. prepare emulsion for warmer hypo and wash water

14. Which one of the following is NOT found in developer?   14._____
    A. Metol   B. Hydroxyquinone
    C. Hydroquinone   D. Sodium carbonate

15. A common preservative in developers to prolong life is sodium   15._____
    A. thiosulphite   B. alpha sulphite
    C. sulphate   D. sulphite

16. Sodium carbonate is used as a component of developer to   16._____
    A. soften black tones   B. harden black tones
    C. retard hydroquinone   D. soften emulsion

17. Which one of the following is NOT found in fixor?   17._____
    A. Sodium hyposulphite   B. Sodium monosulphite
    C. Alum   D. Sodium sulphite

18. The MOST economical way to cool developer is to   18._____
    A. add ice or cold water to solution
    B. add ice or cold water to surrounding bath
    C. blow a fan over surface of tank
    D. add powdered developer to solution

19. The life of developer depends in part on all of the following EXCEPT   19._____
    A. temperature   B. dark room ventilation
    C. age   D. number of films processed

20. Film fog is NOT produced by   20._____
    A. hot developer
    B. exposure of leaded cassette to stray radiation
    C. a safe light that is too strong
    D. failure to use a short stop bath

21. Use of a warm developer will NOT result in
    A. reduced contrast
    B. softened emulsion
    C. under-exposure
    D. lengthened fixing period

22. Replenishers will keep the tank level up but will NOT
    A. shorten developing time
    B. renew and prolong developer life
    C. prevent oxidation
    D. give contrast

23. Alum is used in fixer to
    A. hasten fixing time
    B. give better contrast
    C. preserve and harden emulsion
    D. shorten washing time

24. Solutions, when not in use, should be covered to prevent each of the following EXCEPT
    A. evaporation
    B. contamination
    C. oxidation
    D. expansion

25. PRIMARILY, colored paper is left on films used in cardboard to prevent
    A. static marks
    B. "nail defects"
    C. fogging if cardboard is not light-tight
    D. scratching

26. Developer is added to developer to
    A. speed up developer
    B. maintain tank level
    C. prevent oxidation
    D. delay reduction

27. Hypo is NOT used to
    A. speed processing
    B. remove all silver salts
    C. preserve emulsion
    D. chemically neutralize film prior to washing

28. With new developer, the time of development is controlled DIRECTLY by
    A. number of films
    B. film exposure
    C. temperature of bath
    D. film area

29. Developers become weak through each of the following EXCEPT
    A. hydration   B. saturation   C. oxidation   D. induction

30. A good way to make a rough estimate of hypo deterioration is based on a rule of thumb which provides that hypo is expended when, compared with new solution, the old solution takes ____ time as long to clear a film.
    A. 3   B. 6   C. 9   D. 12

Questions 31-50.

DIRECTIONS: Questions 31 through 50 consist of statements. You are to decide whether each statement is true or false. If the statement is true or correct, print the letter T; if the statement is false or incorrect, print the letter F.

31. A roentgen ray is the same as an x-ray. 31._____

32. A Coolidge tube is *primarily* a form of rectifying tube. 32._____

33. An x-ray machine is *more likely* to spark in cold, dry weather. 33._____

34. A stationary grid is used to cut down secondary radiation effect on a film. 34._____

35. A rheostat is a form of darkroom timer. 35._____

36. A Lysholm grid is a device for partially eliminating secondary radiation effect from a film. 36._____

37. The number of watts in a circuit is *equal* to the volts multiplied by the amperes. 37._____

38. Chest films should *never* be taken in the antero-posterior projection. 38._____

39. The closer a structure is to a cassette, the greater is the degree of distortion of its image, all other factors remaining constant. 39._____

40. In tomography, the cassette moves during the exposure. 40._____

41. A small intestinal study is obtained in every barium clysma. 41._____

42. A prone pressure device is *frequently* employed in urinary tract work. 42._____

43. The aorta is a large artery. 43._____

44. The right lung *normally* has fewer lobes than the left lung. 44._____

45. The dorsal spine is the same as thoracic spine. 45._____

46. Darkroom tunnels or light traps should be painted white so the technician can see better. 46._____

47. On film processing, the exposed film is first put in hypo and then in the developer. 47._____

48. The chemical name for hypo is hydroquinone. 48._____

49. After fixing, x-ray films should be washed for from 15 to 30 minutes. 49._____

50. Films which are sensitive to x-rays are *not* sensitive to ordinary light. 50._____

KEY (CORRECT ANSWERS)

1. A	11. D	21. C	31. T	41. F
2. A	12. B	22. C	32. F	42. F
3. D	13. A	23. C	33. F	43. T
4. C	14. B	24. D	34. T	44. F
5. D	15. D	25. C	35. F	45. T
6. C	16. D	26. B	36. T	46. F
7. C	17. B	27. A	37. T	47. F
8. C	18. B	28. C	38. F	48. F
9. B	19. B	29. D	39. F	49. T
10. C	20. D	30. A	40. T	50. F

EXAMINATION SECTION
TEST 1

DIRECTIONS: Each question or incomplete statement is followed by several suggested answers or completions. Select the one that BEST answers the question or completes the statement. *PRINT THE LETTER OF THE CORRECT ANSWER IN THE SPACE AT THE RIGHT.*

1. Which of the following is the APPROXIMATE skin dose, in rads, for 10 minutes of fluoroscopy performed at 1.5 mA? 1.____

    A. 10 B. 15 C. 20 D. 30

2. Which of the following would MOST likely cause a decrease in patient exposure? 2.____

    A. Increasing kVp 15% and cutting mAs in half
    B. Two tomographic cuts instead of two plain films
    C. Changing from a non-grid technique to an 8:1 grid
    D. Changing from a 400 film/screen combination to a 200 film/screen combination

3. Undifferentiated cells are 3.____

    A. highly radiosensitive
    B. immature
    C. without a specific function
    D. all of the above

4. Which of the following is LEAST radiosensitive? 4.____

    A. Blood forming cells   B. Nerves
    C. Lens   D. Gonads

5. The effects of radiation exposure are dependent upon the 5.____

    A. amount of radiation
    B. size of the irradiated area
    C. length of exposure
    D. all of the above

6. The occupational MPD is valid for all of the following rays EXCEPT 6.____

    A. alpha B. beta C. gamma D. x-rays

7. A greater Linear Energy Transfer (LET) is delivered by particles with a velocity and _____ charge. 7.____

    A. faster; greater   B. slower; greater
    C. faster; lesser   D. slower; lesser

8. As the amount of Linear Energy Transfer increases (from interaction occurring between radiation and biologic material), the amount of biologic effect or damage will 8.____

    A. remain the same   B. decrease
    C. increase   D. not be calculable

9. Follow-up studies have been done on individuals receiving accidental exposure to radiation. Pioneer radiation workers have been shown to have a GREATER incidence of _____ compared with the normal population.

   A. leukemia and other cancers
   B. cataract formation
   C. shortened life span
   D. all of the above

10. _____ is the single BEST method of protecting a patient from excessive radiation.

    A. Shielding   B. Pulsing
    C. Beam restriction   D. All of the above

11. The radiation exposure of a patient receiving an entrance dose of 400 mR at 1 meter is _____ mR.

    A. 0.4   B. 4.0   C. 40   D. 400

12. If an infant cannot be held by mechanical restraints, all of the following may be used to assist EXCEPT a

    A. friend of the family   B. relative
    C. radiology employee   D. nurse

13. All of the following positions can demonstrate the air-fluid level in an infant EXCEPT

    A. recumbent AP   B. erect
    C. decubitus   D. none of the above

14. The formation of electrons within the x-ray tube is accomplished by

    A. induction   B. thermionic emission
    C. conduction   D. all of the above

15. With three-phase equipment, the voltage never drops to zero, and x-ray intensity is significantly

    A. less   B. unchanged   C. greater   D. lost

16. Proper care of leaded apparel includes

    A. not folding lead aprons or gloves after use
    B. hanging lead aprons on an appropriate rack after use
    C. annual fluoroscopy of aprons and gloves to check for cracks
    D. all of the above

17. All of the following statements are true regarding tracheostomy patients EXCEPT:

    A. The tracheostomy patient will have difficulty speaking
    B. A gurgling or rattling sound coming from the trachea indicates the need for suctioning
    C. Any movement of the tracheostomy tube will not cause obstruction of the airway
    D. Rotation of the tracheostomy tube may cause the tube to become dislodged

18. When multiple films are taken on a patient, each radiograph must include all of the following information EXCEPT the

    A. right or left side marker
    B. patient's name or ID number
    C. time and date of the examination
    D. patient's birthdate

19. The MOST common adverse reaction of a patient receiving iodinated contrast medium is

    A. severe headache   B. fever
    C. hives   D. abdominal pain

20. Fractures of the humerus and shoulder girdle are quite painful due to difficulties in immobilizing the upper extremities.
    All of the following are true statements regarding the radiographic examination of such patients EXCEPT:

    A. They should be performed as quickly as possible
    B. They should be performed with the fewest number of changes in body position
    C. The best position is upright
    D. PA and left lateral decubitus must be taken

21. A complete patient history is required prior to injection of an iodinated contrast medium. The patient should be questioned regarding

    A. allergy history
    B. asthma and hay fever history
    C. previous reactions to contrast media
    D. all of the above

22. Areas of the body that are susceptible to bed sores or decubitus ulcers include all of the following EXCEPT the

    A. scapulae   B. trochanters
    C. toes   D. sacrum

23. A patient undergoing radiographic examination starts to experience a seizure. You should

    A. continue taking the x-rays
    B. stop the radiography and give a sedative
    C. stop the radiography and protect the patient from hitting any hard surfaces or falling off the examination table
    D. stop the radiography and wait for the seizure to end

24. The intraspinal method of contrast medium administration is used in myelography and may be performed in the _____ position.

    A. seated   B. lateral
    C. prone   D. all of the above

25. Aseptic techniques used for the administration of contrast media are given via

   A. oral route
   B. rectal route
   C. nasogastric tube
   D. all of the above

KEY (CORRECT ANSWERS)

1. D
2. A
3. D
4. B
5. D

6. A
7. B
8. C
9. D
10. C

11. A
12. C
13. A
14. B
15. C

16. D
17. C
18. D
19. C
20. D

21. D
22. C
23. C
24. D
25. D

TEST 2

DIRECTIONS: Each question or incomplete statement is followed by several suggested answers or completions. Select the one that BEST answers the question or completes the statement. *PRINT THE LETTER OF THE CORRECT ANSWER IN THE SPACE AT THE RIGHT.*

1. When the antecubital vein is inaccessible, the _____ vein is used to administer contrast media. 1.____

    A. basilic B. cephalic C. femoral D. ulnar

2. The movement of a synovial joint that decreases the angle between articulating surfaces is called 2.____

    A. protraction
    C. flexion
    B. adduction
    D. extension

3. After a barium enema examination, the patient should be instructed to 3.____

    A. increase intake of fluid and fiber
    B. monitor bowel movements and have at least one in the next 24 hours
    C. expect white colored stool until all barium is expelled
    D. all of the above

4. Cyanosis resulting from oxygen deficiency is characterized by a bluish discoloration of the 4.____

    A. gums
    C. nail beds
    B. lips
    D. all of the above

5. All of the following are iodinated contrast media EXCEPT 5.____

    A. metrizamide
    C. ethiodized oil
    B. barium sulfate
    D. meglumine diatrizoate

6. Barium sulfate may be used for GI radiography in all of the following clinical conditions EXCEPT 6.____

    A. perforation of the gastrointestinal tract
    B. GI polyps
    C. colorectal cancer
    D. pancreatitis

7. Shock occurs when blood pressure is unable to provide sufficient oxygenated blood to body tissues. 7.____
   Common symptoms of shock include

    A. a drop in blood pressure
    B. increased pulse rate
    C. restlessness and apprehension
    D. all of the above

8. The protrusion of a portion of an organ through a wall that normally contains it is called a(n)

   A. extravasation
   B. herniation
   C. diverticulosis
   D. excretion

9. It is the radiographer's responsibility to provide the radiologist with all of the following EXCEPT

   A. films of diagnostic quality
   B. pertinent patient history
   C. diagnosis and prognosis
   D. none of the above

10. Substances or chemicals that retard the growth of pathogenic bacteriae, but do not necessarily kill them, are termed

    A. germicides
    B. disinfectants
    C. antiseptics
    D. toxins

11. All of the following parts of the gastrointestinal tract can be shown through oral administration of barium sulfate EXCEPT the

    A. esophagus
    B. stomach
    C. sigmoid colon
    D. small bowel

12. The consent given by a patient upon admission to the hospital is sufficient for all of the following radio-graphic examinations EXCEPT

    A. chest x-ray
    B. renal arteriogram
    C. abdominal x-rays
    D. sialography

13. All of the following are advantages of low-osmolality and non-ionic water soluble contrast media over ionic contrast media EXCEPT:

    A. They are less costly
    B. Allergic reactions are less likely
    C. They can be used for intrathecal and intravascular injections
    D. Side effects are less severe

14. The *recumbent* position means lying

    A. on the back
    B. face downward
    C. down in any position
    D. down with a horizontal x-ray beam

15. The position in which the body is rotated with the left anterior portion closest to the film is called the _____ oblique.

    A. right anterior
    B. left anterior
    C. right posterior
    D. left posterior

16. Which of the following should be done prior to bringing the patient into the x-ray examination room?

    A. Clean the x-ray table
    B. Prepare the room for the examination to be performed
    C. Make sure that the x-ray room is clean and orderly
    D. All of the above

17. A fracture caused by a fall onto an outstretched hand in order to *brake* a fall is called a _____ fracture.

    A. greenstick   B. Colles'
    C. Salter   D. none of the above

18. The thorax is composed of the

    A. 12 pairs of ribs   B. sternum
    C. thoracic vertebrae D. all of the above

19. The lateral elbow and lateral forearm must be flexed 90° in order to superimpose all of the following EXCEPT the

    A. distal radius   B. distal ulna
    C. humeral epicondyles D. medial ulna

20. The sacroiliac joints angle posteriorly and medially 25° to the mid sagittal plane. In order to show them with the patient in the AP position, the affected side must be elevated

    A. 20°   B. 25°   C. 50°   D. 75°

21. In which of the following projections would the greater tubercle be seen in profile?

    A. AP humerus   B. Lateral humerus
    C. AP elbow   D. Lateral elbow

22. Small amounts of fluid are BEST demonstrated in the

    A. lateral decubitus position, affected side up
    B. lateral decubitus position, affected side down
    C. lateral recumbent position
    D. prone position

23. Small amounts of air are BEST demonstrated in the _____ if the erect position cannot be obtained.

    A. lateral decubitus position, affected side up
    B. lateral recumbent position, affected side down
    C. AP Trendelenberg position
    D. lateral recumbent position

24. Full or forced expiration is used to elevate the diaphragm and demonstrate the   24.____

    A. ribs above the diaphragm
    B. ribs above the diaphragm, while obliterating pulmonary vascular markings
    C. ribs below the diaphragm to best advantage
    D. heart

25. Shallow breathing technique is occasionally used to visualize   25.____

    A. above the diaphragm ribs
    B. below the diaphragm ribs
    C. pulmonary vascular marking
    D. cardiac vessels

KEY (CORRECT ANSWERS)

1. A
2. C
3. D
4. D
5. B

6. A
7. D
8. B
9. C
10. C

11. C
12. B
13. A
14. C
15. B

16. D
17. B
18. D
19. D
20. B

21. A
22. B
23. A
24. C
25. A

EXAMINATION SECTION

TEST 1

DIRECTIONS: Each question or incomplete statement is followed by several suggested answers or completions. Select the one that BEST answers the question or completes the statement. *PRINT THE LETTER OF THE CORRECT ANSWER IN THE SPACE AT THE RIGHT.*

1. Which of the following groups of exposure factors will produce the GREATEST radiographic density?
   A. 100mA, 0.03s, 36-in SID
   B. 100mA, 0.06s, 36-in SID
   C. 200mA, 0.03s, 72-in SID
   D. 200mA, 0.06s, 72-in SID

1.____

2. Which of the following groups of exposure factors would be MOST appropriate to control involuntary motion?
   A. 100mA, 0.12s
   B. 200mA, 0.06s
   C. 400mA, 0.03s
   D. 600mA, 0.02s

2.____

3. When dealing with involuntary motion, you may cut exposure time in half if you increase kVp by what factor?
   A. 15%   B. 25%   C. 35%   D. 50%

3.____

4. What is the PRIMARY purpose of the circulation system for an automatic processor?
   A. Ensure chemicals are at the appropriate fill levels.
   B. Ensure proper film exposure.
   C. Ensure proper operating temperature.
   D. Agitate, mix, and filter solutions.

4.____

5. All of the following are purposes for a radiology quality assurance program EXCEPT:
   A. Ensure efficiency of x-ray equipment
   B. Maintain quality of radiologic exams
   C. Ensure competency of radiology staff
   D. Minimize radiation dose to patients

5.____

6. Which of the following provides the PRIMARY source of scattered radiation?
   A. X-ray tube   B. Patient   C. Tabletop   D. Grid

6.____

7. The film presented at the right is an example of what type of error?
   A. Motion
   B. Double exposure
   C. Focal spot blur
   D. Poor screen/film contact

7.____

8. What medical condition would require the x-ray technologist to increase the exposure factors?
   A. Ascites
   B. Bowel obstruction
   C. Pneumothorax
   D. Renal colic

9. The _____ is defined as the variation in photon distribution between the anode and cathode ends of the x-ray tube.
   A. Bohr's Theory
   B. The Inverse Square Law
   C. The Anode Heel Effect
   D. The Line Focus Principle

10. Which of the following are materials that emit light when stimulated by x-ray photons?
    A. Ions
    B. Electrodes
    C. Crystals
    D. Phosphors

11. Which of the following can be a cause of foreshortening?
    A. Excessive distance between the focus and the film
    B. Insufficient distance between the focus and the film
    C. The radiographic object being placed at an angle to the film
    D. Excessive distance between the object and the film

12. The image shown at the right depicts what type of image artifact?
    A. Inverted focused grid
    B. Poor screen/film contact
    C. Foreign bodies
    D. Static electricity

13. _____ can affect the amount of replenisher delivered per film in an automatic processor.
    A. Film size
    B. Developer temperature
    C. Processor capacity
    D. Amount of film exposure

14. All of the following affect the exposure rate of the primary beam EXCEPT
    A. field size
    B. mA
    C. kVp
    D. distance

15. Which of the following is the PRIMARY regulator of the number of photons delivered to a patient in a given exposure?
    A. Focal spot size
    B. SID
    C. kVp
    D. mAs

16. In what manner should unopened boxes of radiographic film be stored?
    A. Away from radiation in the vertical position
    B. Away from radiation in the horizontal position
    C. Stacked with the newest on top
    D. Stacked with the oldest on top

16.____

17. _____ are responsible for changing exposed silver halide crystals to black metallic silver.
    A. Activators   B. Reducers
    C. Preservatives   D. Hardeners

17.____

18. _____ is added to the developer to prevent excessive softening of the emulsion and prevent the film from sticking to the processor rollers.
    A. Potassium bromide   B. Ammonium thiosulfate
    C. Hydroquinone   D. Glutaraldehyde

18.____

19. All of the following are factors that may contribute to film fog EXCEPT
    A. storage in a cool environment   B. age of the film
    C. excessive exposure to safelight   D. imbalanced processor chemistry

19.____

20. All of the following can influence x-ray photon beam attenuation EXCEPT
    A. photon quality   B. subject thickness
    C. tissue type   D. photon quantity

20.____

21. _____ is defined as the reduction in x-ray photon intensity as the photon passes through material.
    A. Divergence   B. Scattering
    C. Attenuation   D. Absorption

21.____

22. A _____ functions to produce a uniform density on an x-ray image.
    A. Compensating filter   B. Intensifying screen
    C. Grid   D. Penetrometer

22.____

23. For what reason is a very short exposure time necessary when taking a chest x-ray?
    A. Minimize patient discomfort   B. Minimize patient motion
    C. Avoid excessive focal spot blur D. Maintain short-scale contrast

23.____

24. What would be the APPROXIMATE density for an unexposed film that has been processed?
    A. 0.0   B. 0.1   C. 1.0   D. 2.5

24.____

25. _____ is defined as light being reflected from one intensifying screen, through the film, to the opposite emulsion and screen.
    A. Filtration   B. Scatter   C. Crossover   D. Reflectance

25.____

KEY (CORRECT ANSWERS)

1. B
2. D
3. A
4. D
5. C

6. B
7. B
8. A
9. C
10. D

11. C
12. D
13. A
14. A
15. D

16. A
17. B
18. D
19. A
20. D

21. C
22. A
23. B
24. B
25. C

TEST 2

DIRECTIONS: Each question or incomplete statement is followed by several suggested answers or completions. Select the one that BEST answers the question or completes the statement. *PRINT THE LETTER OF THE CORRECT ANSWER IN THE SPACE AT THE RIGHT.*

1. Which method would be APPROPRIATE for demonstrating blowout fractures of the orbit?
    A. Lateral projection of the facial bones
    B. Posteroanterior projection with the 15° caudal angle
    C. Sweet's localization method
    D. Water's method

2. Which view would you use to demonstrate on of the paranasal sinuses?
    A. True PA
    B. True AP
    C. Lateral
    D. Parietocanthial

3. The _____ flexure is the junction of the transverse colon and the descending colon.
    A. hepatic
    B. sigmoid
    C. splenic
    D. transverse

4. Which form of contrast media would be the MOST appropriate for performing myelography?
    A. Gas
    B. Nonionic water-soluble
    C. Ionic water-soluble
    D. Ionic non-water-soluble

5. Which views of the shoulder would be APPROPRIATE for ruling out a fracture?
    A. AP and scapular Y
    B. AP and AP axial
    C. AP and tangential
    D. Internal and external rotation

6. Which medical condition can be visualized with the use of an AP Trendelenburg position during an upper GI exam?
    A. Pyloric stenosis
    B. Gastroparesis
    C. Bleeding varices
    D. Hiatal hernia

7. _____ is defined as an occluded blood vessel inhibiting blood flow to a portion of the lungs.
    A. Hypoxia
    B. Pneumothorax
    C. Atelectasis
    D. Pulmonary embolism

8. The view of the _____ foot would be BEST for demonstrating the sinus tarsi, cuboid, and tuberosity of the fifth metatarsal.
    A. weight-bearing
    B. lateral
    C. medial oblique
    D. lateral oblique

9. _____ fracture is described as a small bony fragment pulled from a bony process.
   A. Avulsion
   B. Torus
   C. Comminuted
   D. Compound

10. All of the following landmarks associated with pelvic radiography are palpable EXCEPT
    A. iliac crest
    B. greater trochanter
    C. public symphysis
    D. femoral neck

11. _____ is defined as the inhalation of liquid or solid particles into the nose, throat, or lungs.
    A. Asphyxia
    B. Aspiration
    C. Atelectasis
    D. Aphagia

12. What type of fracture, with associated treatment, is depicted in the radiograph shown at the right?
    A. Talus
    B. Torus
    C. Comminuted
    D. Compound

13. What type of articulation is evaluated through the use of arthrography?
    A. Synarthrodal
    B. Diarthrodal
    C. Amphiarthrodal
    D. Cartilagenous

14. Ureteral reflux would be BEST visualized during which radiological examination?
    A. Voiding cystourethrogram
    B. Retrograde pyelogram
    C. Intravenous urogram
    D. Nephrotomogram

15. Which radiological procedure would prove beneficial for dilating a stenotic vessel?
    A. Surgical nephrostomy
    B. Renal arteriography
    C. Percutaneous angioplasty
    D. Percutaneous nephrolithotomy

16. Which medical condition is depicted in the radiograph shown at the right?
    A. Pneumonia
    B. Emphysema
    C. Pneumothorax
    D. Pleural effusion

17. Which of the following is the MOST effective method for controlling voluntary motion during a radiology procedure?
    A. Physical restraint
    B. Immobilization of the affected body part
    C. Decrease exposure time
    D. Careful and precise explanation of the procedure

18. The _____ is the ridge that marks the bifurcation of the trachea into the right and left primary bronchi.
    A. alveoli   B. hilus   C. carina   D. epiglottis

19. All of the following bones participate in the formation of the acetabulum EXCEPT
    A. femoral head   B. ilium   C. ischium   D. pubis

20. Which of the following is used to locate peripheral lymphatic vessels?
    A. Water-soluble iodinated contrast media
    B. Blue dye
    C. Ethiodized oil
    D. Ionic non-water-soluble contrast media

21. Which of the following structures is located in the right lower quadrant?
    A. Cecum   B. Gallbladder
    C. Hepatic flexure   D. Descending colon

22. Which of the following radiographic procedures is performed by administering radiopaque contrast media through a uttering cannula?
    A. Myelogram   B. Retrograde pyelogram
    C. Hysterosalpingogram   D. Voiding cystourethrogram

23. All of the following bones are associated with condyles EXCEPT
    A. mandible   B. fibula   C. tibia   D. femur

24. Which view is depicted on the pediatric radiograph shown at the right?
    A. Right lateral decubitus
    B. Left lateral decubitus
    C. Dorsal decubitus
    D. Ventral decubitus

25. Which of the following projections would be MOST effective for isolating the gallbladder from the vertebrae in an asthenic patient? 25._____
    A. LAO B. RAO C. LPO D. RPO

KEY (CORRECT ANSWERS)

1. D
2. C
3. C
4. C
5. A

6. D
7. D
8. C
9. A
10. D

11. B
12. A
13. B
14. A
15. C

16. B
17. D
18. C
19. A
20. B

21. A
22. C
23. B
24. B
25. A

TEST 3

DIRECTIONS: Each question or incomplete statement is followed by several suggested answers or completions. Select the one that BEST answers the question or completes the statement. *PRINT THE LETTER OF THE CORRECT ANSWER IN THE SPACE AT THE RIGHT.*

1. What position should the patient be placed in order to properly demonstrate esophageal varices? 1.____
   A. Erect
   B. Prone
   C. Recumbent
   D. Fowler's position

2. Which of the following anatomical structures lies proximal to the carpal bones? 2.____
   A. Radial styloid process
   B. Proximal interphalangeal joints
   C. Distal interphalangeal joints
   D. Metacarpals

3. The _____ position is characterized by the patient being recumbent and the central ray being directed horizontally. 3.____
   A. Sims
   B. Trendelenburg
   C. Fowler's
   D. Decubitus

4. Which position would MOST effectively demonstrate apophyseal articulations of the lumbar vertebrae? 4.____
   A. PA   B. Left lateral   C. RPO   D. LPO

5. The pedicule is represented by which part of the "scotty dog" as seen in the correctly positioned radiograph of the oblique lumbar spine. 5.____
   A. Neck
   B. Body
   C. Eye
   D. Front foot

6. At what level do the carotid arteries bifurcate? 6.____
   A. C1   B. C4   C. Trachea   D. Pharynx

7. All of the following statements are TRUE regarding positioning of pediatric patients EXCEPT:
   A. For renal examinations, the central ray should be directed midway between the diaphragm and the symphysis pubis
   B. Patients with a myelomeningocele defect should be performed in the supine position
   C. For neonates, chest x-rays should be obtained in the supine position
   D. If patient is in respiratory distress, chest x-rays should be obtained in the AP rather than standard PA projection

8. Which of the following radiological procedures MUST be performed with an intrathecal injection?
   A. Intravenous pyelogram
   B. Retrograde pyelogram
   C. Arthrogram
   D. Myelogram

9. The ileocecal valve is normally located in which region of the body?
   A. Hypograstric
   B. Right lumbar
   C. Right iliac
   D. Left iliac

10. All of the following statements are true regarding respiratory structures EXCEPT:
    A. The uppermost portion of the lung is the apex
    B. Each lung is enclosed in pleura
    C. The right lung has two lobes
    D. The trachea bifurcates into mainstem bronchi

11. The term _____ refers to parts closer to the source or beginning.
    A. proximal   B. medial   C. caudad   D. cephalad

12. What skull position will adequately demonstrate the cranial base, sphenoidal sinuses, atlas, and odontoid process?
    A. AP axial
    B. Lateral
    C. Submentovertical
    D. Partietocanthial

13. Which of the following bony landmarks is in the same transverse plane as the symphysis pubis?
    A. Ischial tuberosity
    B. Greater trochanter
    C. Anterior superior iliac spine
    D. Anterior inferior iliac spine

14. _____ is the tissue that occupies the central cavity within the shaft on a long bone in an adult.
    A. Cancellous tissue
    B. Cortical tissue
    C. Yellow marrow
    D. Red marrow

15. Which of the following would be the MOST likely projections for a routine examination of the forearm?
    A. PA and medial oblique
    B. AP and lateral oblique
    C. PA and lateral
    D. AP and lateral

16. The _____ is the portion of the long bone where cartilage has been replaced by bone.
    A. metaphysis B. epiphysis C. diaphysis D. apophysis

17. What hormone is secreted by the duodenal mucosa after eating a fatty meal to stimulate the contraction of the gallbladder?
    A. Pepsin
    B. Insulin
    C. Cholecystokinin
    D. Gastrin

18. _____ is a major cause of bowel obstruction among children.
    A. Intussusception
    B. Appendicitis
    C. Regional enteritis
    D. Ulcerative colitis

19. Which of the following medical conditions is often the result of ureteral obstruction or stricture?
    A. Cystourethritis
    B. Hydronephrosis
    C. Nephroptosis
    D. Pyelonephrosis

20. All of the following are components of a trimalleolar fracture EXCEPT fractured
    A. fibula
    B. posterior tibia
    C. lateral malleolus
    D. medical malleolus

21. _____ is the medical condition that results in the forward slipping of one vertebra on the vertebra below.
    A. Spondylosis
    B. Spondyloslisthesis
    C. Spondylolysis
    D. Spondylitis

22. Which of the following statements is TRUE regarding the appropriate method to demonstrate contrast filled distal ureters during IV urography?
    A. Use a 15° AP Trendelenburg position
    B. Use a 30° AP Trendelenburg position
    C. Apply compression to the proximal ureters
    D. Apply compression to the distal ureters

23. Which radiographic exam involves fluoroscopic imaging of the ileocecal valve?
    A. ERCP
    B. Barium enema
    C. Small-bowel series
    D. Upper-GI series

24. What type of fracture is illustrated in the radiograph shown at the right?
    A. Avulsion fracture
    B. Torus fracture
    C. Comminuted fracture
    D. Compound fracture

25. _____ is defined as movement of a part toward the midline of the body. 25._____
   A. Pronation   B. Supination   C. Adduction   D. Abduction

---

KEY (CORRECT ANSWERS)

1.	C	11.	A
2.	A	12.	C
3.	D	13.	B
4.	D	14.	C
5.	C	15.	D
6.	B	16.	A
7.	B	17.	C
8.	D	18.	A
9.	C	19.	B
10.	C	20.	A

21. B
22. A
23. C
24. D
25. C

TEST 4

DIRECTIONS: Each question or incomplete statement is followed by several suggested answers or completions. Select the one that BEST answers the question or completes the statement. *PRINT THE LETTER OF THE CORRECT ANSWER IN THE SPACE AT THE RIGHT.*

1. Which type of timer functions to accurately duplicate radiographic densities?
   A. Phototimer
   B. Electronic timer
   C. Synchronous timer
   D. Impulse timer

2. Which of the following is the PRIMARY function of a photomultiplier?
   A. Provide a brighter fluoroscopic image
   B. Automatically restrict field size
   C. Automatically increase or decrease incoming line voltages
   D. Terminate the x-ray exposure once the image receptor is correctly exposed

3. When performing fluoroscopy, what does the automatic brightness control adjust?
   A. kVp and mA
   B. Backup timer
   C. mA and time
   D. kVp and time

4. Which piece of equipment is mandatory for performing a myelogram?
   A. Tomography
   B. Tilting x-ray table
   C. Cine camera
   D. 105-mm spot film

5. _____ radiation is that which emerges from the patient to form a radiographic image.
   A. Primary   B. Scattered   C. Secondary   D. Remnant

6. _____ is a technique that is used to evaluate the dynamics of a body part or organ.
   A. Stereoscopy   B. Fluoroscopy   C. Tomography   D. Phototiming

7. Which of the following describes the chemical ionization effects of an electric current?
   A. Induction   B. Rectification   C. Electrolysis   D. Phoresis

8. When performing cinefluorography, at what point is the camera shutter open?
   A. Between frames
   B. When the film adjusts
   C. During exposures
   D. Constantly

9. What is used to test the congruence of the x-ray beam with the light field?
   A. Radiopaque objects
   B. Pinhole camera
   C. Star pattern
   D. Slit camera

10. Which modality within the field of radiology would benefit from an extended film process of three minutes?
    A. Mammography
    B. Macroradiology
    C. Computed tomography
    D. Computed radiography

11. The basic operation of which procedure involves the reciprocal motion of the x-ray tube and film?
    A. Tomography
    B. Fluoroscopy
    C. Spectroscopy
    D. Cinefluorography

12. What is the result from the transitioning of orbital electrons from outer to inner shells?
    A. Characteristic radiation
    B. Bremsstrahlung radiation
    C. Scattered radiation
    D. Remnant radiation

13. What is the result of a high-speed electron entering the tungsten target being attracted to the positive nucleus of a tungsten atom and is decelerated in the process?
    A. Characteristic radiation
    B. Bremsstrahlung radiation
    C. Scattered radiation
    D. Remnant radiation

14. Which of the following is a universally accepted standard for exchanging medical imaging studies via a networked set of display workstations, archive, and imaging modalities?
    A. PACS   B. DICOM   C. HIPAA   D. HL-7

15. _____ is used to describe the reading of images outside of the hospital walls, generally at home or in remote locations.
    A. Teleradiology
    B. Virtual radiology
    C. Macroradiology
    D. Microradiology

16. Who should be responsible for annual testing and acceptance testing of all radiologic imaging equipment?
    A. Technologist
    B. Physician
    C. Physicist
    D. Biomedical engineer

17. _____ refers to a comprehensive set of activities designed to monitor and maintain a piece of equipment.
    A. Continuous quality improvement
    B. Quality assurance
    C. Quality control
    D. Quality expectance

18. How often should preventative maintenance be performed on all radiological devices?
    A. Weekly   B. Monthly   C. Biannually   D. Annually

19. All of the following pieces of information are required to be included on every x-ray film EXCEPT
    A. patient's name/ID number
    B. date of the exam
    C. patient date of birth
    D. orientation markers

20. All of the following statements are true regarding proper hand hygiene techniques EXCEPT:
    A. Keep hands and forearms lower than the elbows
    B. Use paper towels to turn water on
    C. Avoid using hand lotions whenever possible
    D. Carefully wash all surfaces including between the fingers

21. For intravenous contrast agents, which of the following is defined as the total number of dissolved particles in solution per kilogram of water?
    A. Miscibility   B. Viscosity   C. Solubility   D. Osmolality

22. What is the appropriate protocol for dealing with patients with Foley catheter bags?
    Drainage bag should be
    A. placed above the level of the bladder
    B. placed at the same level as the bladder
    C. placed below the level of the bladder
    D. clamped during the radiological procedure

23. A patient is ordered an Upper GI, an IVP, and a barium enema. In what order should these exams be performed to ensure optimum image quality?
    A. Barium enema, Upper GI, IVP
    B. Upper GI, barium enema, IVP
    C. IVP, Upper GI, barium enema
    D. IVP, barium enema, Upper GI

24. All of the following factors are important to evaluate when selecting contrast media EXCEPT
    A. miscibility   B. toxicity   C. solubility   D. viscosity

25. According to the Centers for Disease Control and Prevention, all of the following bodily fluids should be treated as if they contained pathogenic microorganisms EXCEPT
    A. blood
    B. urine
    C. synovial fluid
    D. cerebrospinal fluid

KEY (CORRECT ANSWERS)

1. A
2. D
3. A
4. B
5. D

6. B
7. C
8. C
9. A
10. B

11. A
12. A
13. B
14. B
15. A

16. C
17. C
18. C
19. C
20. C

21. D
22. C
23. D
24. C
25. D

EXAMINATION SECTION
TEST 1

DIRECTIONS: Each question or incomplete statement is followed by several suggested answers or completions. Select the one that BEST answers the question or completes the statement. *PRINT THE LETTER OF THE CORRECT ANSWER IN THE SPACE AT THE RIGHT.*

1. For an intravenous cholangiogram, the area of the abdomen which you should radiograph is the _____ quadrant.

    A. left upper
    B. left lower
    C. right upper
    D. right lower

2. The ilium is part of the

    A. pelvis
    B. small intestine
    C. colon
    D. pancreas

3. The olecranon is a part of the

    A. shoulder
    B. knee
    C. hip
    D. elbow

4. The outlet of the bladder is known as the

    A. urethra
    B. ureter
    C. kidney
    D. anus

5. The coracoid process is part of the

    A. pelvis
    B. scapula
    C. forearm
    D. cervical spine

6. The manubrium is part of the

    A. ankle
    B. hip
    C. shoulder
    D. sternum

7. The one of the following glands which is located in the abdominal cavity is the

    A. thymus
    B. pineal
    C. adrenal
    D. pituitary

8. The greater trochanter will be seen on films of the

    A. knee
    B. shoulder
    C. leg
    D. hip

9. The external canthus of the eye should be used as a landmark when taking a(n) _____ view of the _____.

    A. lateral; skull
    B. lateral; sella turcica
    C. lateral; paranasal sinuses
    D. AP; malar bone

10. The one of the following landmarks which should be used when radiographing a patient's abdomen for kidneys, ureters, and bladder (KUB) is the

    A. xiphoid process of the sternum
    B. ischial tuberosities
    C. crest of the ilium
    D. umbilicus

11. To take a PA of the skull, the landmark which should be used is the　　　11.___

    A. cantho-meatal line
    B. external auditory meatus
    C. internal canthus of the eye
    D. petrous pyramid

12. In order to determine the anatomical landmarks for a lateral film of the fifth lumbar vertebra, one should locate the　　　12.___

    A. plane connecting the anterior-superior iliac spines
    B. area just below the top of the iliac crests
    C. pubic symphysis
    D. plane connecting the hips

13. Reid's base line is a landmark used in taking radiographs of the　　　13.___

    A. bony pelvis　　　B. skull
    C. small intestines　　　D. thoracic inlet

14. To take a PA of the chest for the heart, the landmark which should be used is the　　　14.___

    A. coracoid process　　　B. crest of the ilium
    C. 2nd dorsal vertebra　　　D. 9th dorsal vertebra

15. To take an AP of the shoulder, the landmark which should be used is the　　　15.___

    A. coracoid process　　　B. 5th dorsal vertebra
    C. 9th dorsal vertebra　　　D. 7th cervical vertebra

16. In radiography, the term *distal* means MOST NEARLY　　　16.___

    A. farthest from the center of the body
    B. toward the back
    C. toward the head
    D. closest to the center of the body

17. In radiography, the term *cephalad* means MOST NEARLY toward the　　　17.___

    A. front　　　B. head　　　C. center　　　D. feet

18. A tunnel view of the knee should be made with the knee　　　18.___

    A. rotated medially　　　B. moderately flexed
    C. completely extended　　　D. turned into the lateral

19. The hand should be placed in pronation when taking a(n)　　　19.___

    A. PA of the wrist
    B. AP of the wrist
    C. lateral of the thumb
    D. oblique of the third finger

20. In radiography, the term *caudad* means MOST NEARLY　　　20.___

    A. lying on the stomach　　　B. inverted
    C. toward the head　　　D. toward the feet

21. In order to visualize the extent of the duodenal loop MOST advantageously, the projection should be made

    A. RPO B. AP C. LAO D. RAO

22. In order to visualize the external malleolus of the ankle MOST advantageously, it should be positioned

    A. in the true AP position
    B. in the true lateral position
    C. with the ankle flexed and the leg rotated internally
    D. with the foot extended and the leg rotated externally

23. In order to remove the scapulae from the lung fields when taking a PA radiograph of the chest, the x-ray technician should

    A. angle the tube 15 toward the feet
    B. use a 72-inch target-film distance
    C. roll the patient's shoulders forward
    D. have the patient take a deep breath

24. When doing an intravenous pyelogram, the BEST projection to show both kidneys on a single film is

    A. AP B. PA C. RL D. LAO

25. When all other factors remain unchanged, the density or blackness of the film will vary in _____ proportion to the _____.

    A. *inverse*; time
    B. *inverse*; Kv
    C. *direct*; square of the distance
    D. *inverse*; square of the distance

KEY (CORRECT ANSWERS)

1.	C	11.	A
2.	A	12.	B
3.	D	13.	B
4.	A	14.	D
5.	B	15.	A
6.	D	16.	A
7.	C	17.	B
8.	D	18.	B
9.	C	19.	A
10.	C	20.	D

21. D
22. C
23. C
24. A
25. D

TEST 2

DIRECTIONS: Each question or incomplete statement is followed by several suggested answers or completions. Select the one that BEST answers the question or completes the statement. *PRINT THE LETTER OF THE CORRECT ANSWER IN THE SPACE AT THE RIGHT.*

1. Of the following, it is usually BEST to increase bone contrast in the film by   1.____

   A. increasing Kv B. decreasing time
   C. increasing MaS D. decreasing MaS

2. In a transformer, the Kv may be increased or decreased depending on the ratio of the number of turns of wire in the primary coil to the secondary coil.   2.____
   If there are 100 turns in the primary coil and the secondary has 100,000 turns, then the voltage imparted in the secondary is _____ times _____ than in the primary.

   A. 1000; greater B. 100; greater
   C. 1000; less D. 100,000 greater

3. Assume that, when taking a radiograph, the Kv is increased but the average density remains the same. The contrast will   3.____

   A. remain the same
   B. be increased
   C. be decreased
   D. change in proportion to the change in MaS

4. Of the following, the way to reduce magnification is by the use of   4.____

   A. increased object-film distance
   B. longer target-film distance
   C. shorter target-film distance
   D. a small focal spot

5. If all other factors remain unchanged, the one of the following combinations of time and milliamperes which gives the GREATEST density is _____ second and _____ milliamperes.   5.____

   A. 1/10; 100 B. 1/5; 50
   C. 1/5; 200 D. 1/10; 500

6. Assume that you are checking the accuracy of a timer on a four valve (full-wave) x-ray machine, using a spinning top.   6.____
   If the timer is accurate, the number of dots you should see in a 1/10 second exposure is

   A. 6 B. 12 C. 18 D. 24

7. Assume that the technician, when making a radiograph of the chest, used the usual milliamperage and time settings, but noticed that the MaS recorded on the meter during exposure was only one-half of the setting. The film, when developed, was light.   7.____
   The MOST likely source of the difficulty is the

   A. autotransformer
   B. valve tubes in the rectifier circuit

59

C. line voltage compensator
D. x-ray tube

8. When using portable x-ray machines, an external ground wire is *essential* PRIMARILY because the

   A. machine will operate more efficiently
   B. electrical circuits will be stabilized
   C. hazard of electrical shock will be reduced
   D. machine will not operate without a ground wire

8.____

9. In radiography, a collimator is useful to

   A. increase the output of the x-ray machine
   B. increase the life of the tube
   C. reduce the amount of unnecessary radiation reaching the patient
   D. reduce the exposure time

9.____

10. The function of an autotransformer in an x-ray machine is to control

    A. kilovoltage
    B. milliamperage
    C. time of exposure
    D. rectifying valve tube current

10.____

11. A rapid film changer would be used in

    A. scanography   B. laminography
    C. small intestinal series D. angiocardiography

11.____

12. To get BEST detail when using screen film, the x-ray technician should use the _____ screen.

    A. slow   B. medium
    C. fast   D. extra fast

12.____

13. As compared to the Ma used in equipment for diagnostic radiology, the Ma used in therapy equipment is GENERALLY

    A. higher   B. lower   C. the same   D. varied

13.____

14. Generally, a patient is asked to hold his breath when being x-rayed.
    Of the following, the one which permits quiet shallow breathing, while using a long exposure time and low Ma, is a

    A. cholecystogram
    B. 10 minute film of intravenous pyelogram
    C. PA of the chest
    D. lateral of the dorsal spine

14.____

15. Assume that you are to radiograph a patient's hips utilizing 70 Kv,
    Of the following, the grid ratio which you should select to insure a SATISFACTORY radiograph is

    A. 8:1   B. 10:1   C. 12:1   D. 16:1

15.____

16. Cardboard technique in radiographic work is ESPECIALLY useful for an examination of the

    A. chest   B. skull   C. heart   D. wrist

17. With the patient lying on his side, the x-ray beam should be horizontal when taking a radiograph of the

    A. abdomen to demonstrate fluid level
    B. skull to demonstrate hairline fracture
    C. colon to determine diverticulitis
    D. spine to demonstrate "whiplash" fracture

18. A patient with a clinically diagnosed pneumonia in the right middle lobe is referred to the radiology department for PA and lateral films of the chest.
    The BEST position in which to take the lateral film is

    A. left lateral erect
    B. right lateral
    C. right lateral decubitus with the horizontal beam
    D. right semilateral with the patient rotated 30

19. A thick pasty mixture of barium sulphate and water is USUALLY employed when doing a radiographic examination of the

    A. colon   B. stomach
    C. esophagus   D. small intestine

20. Assume that several patients are scheduled for radiographs of the abdominal region. If the abdomens are of the same thickness and the same Kv is used, the one of the following patients who will usually require the MOST MaS for a good film is a(n)

    A. old woman   B. young woman
    C. cancer patient   D. young man

21. The single view for BEST demonstrating the maxillary sinuses is the

    A. Caldwell   B. Waters
    C. submentovertical   D. Towne

22. In the Stenvers projection (posterior profile view) of the mastoids, the patient faces the film and the head is rotated 45°.
    The tube should be angled toward the vertex of the skull

    A. 5°   B. 12°   C. 25°   D. 45°

23. In the Caldwell (posterior-anterior) projection of the frontal and ethmoid sinuses, the patient faces the film and the orbitomeatal line is perpendicular to the film. The tube should be angled APPROXIMATELY

    A. 15-20° toward the head
    B. 15-20° laterally
    C. 15-20° toward the feet
    D. parallel to the orbitomeatal line

24. The technician is asked to take a film of the left hip of a pregnant woman. It is MOST important to

 A. take a film of the right hip as well for comparison
 B. shield the abdomen
 C. take multiple projections
 D. warn the patient of the possible hazards of radiation

25. In the Law projection (lateral) of the mastoids, the patient is prone and the head is positioned in the true lateral position.
 The central ray enters two inches above and two inches posterior to the external auditory meatus, and the tube is angled _____ toward the _____.

 A. 25°; feet
 B. 10°; feet and 35° toward the face
 C. 25°; face
 D. 15°; feet and 15° toward the face

KEY (CORRECT ANSWERS)

1.	C	11.	D
2.	A	12.	A
3.	C	13.	B
4.	B	14.	D
5.	D	15.	A
6.	B	16.	D
7.	B	17.	A
8.	C	18.	B
9.	C	19.	C
10.	A	20.	D

21.	B
22.	B
23.	C
24.	B
25.	D

PHYSICS & INSTRUMENTATION

EXAMINATION SECTION
TEST 1

DIRECTIONS: Each question or incomplete statement is followed by several suggested answers or completions. Select the one that BEST answers the question or completes the statement. *PRINT THE LETTER OF THE CORRECT ANSWER IN THE SPACE AT THE RIGHT.*

1. The fixed anode tube operates at a typical maximum kilo-voltage of _____ kV. 1.____
   A. 80-100 B. 90-140 C. 100-160 D. 110-180

2. Most of the energy (about 99%) that is generated in an x-ray tube is 2.____
   A. heat
   B. x-ray photons
   C. electrical
   D. none of the above

3. In a CT unit, the post-patient collimation of the x-ray beam assures 3.____
   I. accurate slice thickness
   II. increased spatial resolution
   III. a pencil-like configuration
   The CORRECT answer is:
   A. I, II B. I, III C. II, III D. I, II, III

4. The spectrum of x-rays that are emitted in a CT unit is 4.____
   A. polychromatic
   B. monochromatic
   C. monoenergetic
   D. none of the above

5. The display devices work with _____ signals. 5.____
   A. analog
   B. laser
   C. digital
   D. all of the above

6. The angle of the anode is _____ degrees. 6.____
   A. 10 B. 12 C. 20 D. 25

7. The collimation that is placed between the x-ray beam and the patient is called the _____ collimation. 7.____
   A. post-patient
   B. post-x-ray
   C. pre-patient
   D. x-ray tube

8. The beam hardening effect can be reduced by the use of _____ collimation. 8.____
   A. post-patient
   B. post-x-ray
   C. pre-patient
   D. x-ray tube

9. To maintain the homogeneity of the x-ray beam, _____ is/are commonly used, followed by the ripple filters, to reduce variations in the kV. 9.____
   A. single-phase generators
   B. three-phase generators

C. post-patient collimation
D. pre-patient collimation

10. The amount of light in a _____ is related to the total energy of the x-ray beam.

    A. detector
    B. back-projection
    C. dynode
    D. photomultiplier

11. The x-ray capture efficiency of a crystal detector is NOT related to the crystals'

    A. thickness
    B. density
    C. atomic number
    D. age

12. With a high radiation intensity, sodium iodide crystals have the great disadvantage of

    A. backflash
    B. afterglow
    C. backglow
    D. back-drain

13. The water bag was used in the initial EMI head scanner because

    A. it limited the range of the x-ray beam energies
    B. of the usage of the scintillation crystal-photo-multiplier combination
    C. it decreases the beam hardening effect
    D. all of the above

14. Rapid data accumulation per translation is INCREASED by

    A. a large number of detectors
    B. a large number of photomultipliers
    C. the anode-to-cathode voltage
    D. all of the above

15. The scintillation crystal and the photomultiplier detector system convert transmitted x-ray intensity into

    A. digital signal
    B. electrical signal
    C. binary code
    D. all of the above

16. The electrical signal is converted into a digital signal by a(n)

    A. analog-to-digital converter
    B. digital-to-analog converter
    C. photomultiplier
    D. all of the above

17. Data acquisition is in the form of

    A. analog signals
    B. digital signals
    C. analog data
    D. binary data

18. A finely collimated x-ray beam that greatly reduces scatter to the detector system is called a _____ beam.

    A. parallel
    B. pencil x-ray
    C. fan-shaped
    D. fast-track

19. The analog information must be converted into _____ data before it can be processed by the computer.

    A. reconstruction
    B. digital
    C. binary
    D. digital-analog

20. The average energy of the x-ray beam before entering the patient is APPROXIMATELY _____ keV.

    A. 40-50   B. 50-60   C. 60-70   D. 70-80

21. The changes continuous signal into discrete signals.

    A. digital-to-analog converter
    B. analog converter
    C. analog-to-digital converter
    D. array processor

22. The _____ converter converts the analog signal into a sequence of numbers having finite precision.

    A. digital-to-analog
    B. primary analog
    C. analog-to-digital
    D. digital primary

23. The FIRST step in the production of a CT image is

    A. scan data
    B. raw scan data
    C. x-ray transmission
    D. data acquisition

24. The CT machine is limited to imaging _____ images.

    A. coronal
    B. sagittal
    C. transverse axial
    D. all of the above

25. The exit collimator's PRIMARY purpose is to
    I. decrease patient irradiation
    II. reduce the size of the detector aperture
    III. decrease scattered radiation
    The CORRECT answer is:

    A. I, II   B. I, III   C. II, III   D. I, II, III

KEY (CORRECT ANSWERS)

1. B
2. A
3. B
4. A
5. A

6. B
7. C
8. C
9. B
10. A

11. D
12. B
13. D
14. A
15. B

16. A
17. A
18. B
19. B
20. A

21. C
22. C
23. D
24. C
25. C

TEST 2

DIRECTIONS: Each question or incomplete statement is followed by several suggested answers or completions. Select the one that BEST answers the question or completes the statement. *PRINT THE LETTER OF THE CORRECT ANSWER IN THE SPACE AT THE RIGHT.*

1. A large number of x-ray transmission measurements from different locations are collected when

    A. image data is converted in reformatted images
    B. raw scan data is converted in special reconstructed images
    C. the x-ray tube and detectors rotate around the patient
    D. the DAS and the x-ray tube rotate around the patient

2. The term that refers to the geometric properties of the x-ray beam is called

    A. algorithm B. beam geometry
    C. ionization D. none of the above

3. Beam geometry refers to the _____ x-ray beam.
    I. size and shape of the
    II. shape and motion of the
    III. path traced by the moving
    The CORRECT answer is:

    A. I, II B. I, III C. II, III D. I, II, III

4. A collection of rays for one translation across the object is called

    A. sequence B. view
    C. profile D. none of the above

5. The line from the x-ray tube to the detector is considered a

    A. single ray B. translation
    C. projection D. all of the above

6. The varying of the gray scale to the different CT numbers alters the

    A. contrast B. windows
    C. level D. all of the above

7. A relatively long gray scale range or a large block of CT numbers that will be assigned some value of gray indicates a large

    A. window level B. window width
    C. image contrast D. all of the above

8. A narrow window width is shown by
    I. few CT numbers
    II. large CT numbers
    III. black and white images
    The CORRECT answer is:

    A. I, II B. I, III C. II, III D. I, II, III

9. The center of the gray scale is defined as the

   A. window level
   B. window width
   C. window width and level
   D. image contrast

10. Soft tissues will appear in the middle of the gray scale, the bones will appear white, and the lungs will appear black if the CT number is set at

    A. 1000
    B. 500
    C. 0
    D. -1000

11. A wide gray scale equals a

    A. small range of CT numbers
    B. large range of CT numbers
    C. black and white image
    D. reversed image

12. _____ refers to the collection of x-ray transmission measurements from the patient.

    A. Image display
    B. Data acquisition
    C. Attenuation
    D. Image reconstruction

13. The three-step process of forming CT images is

    A. image reconstruction, data acquisition, image display and manipulation
    B. data acquisition, image display and manipulation, and translation
    C. image reconstruction, data acquisition, and attenuation
    D. data acquisition, translation, image projection

14. When x-rays have passed through the patient, the detectors measure the _____ values.
    I. attenuation
    II. transmission
    III. acquisition
    The CORRECT answer is:

    A. I, II
    B. I, III
    C. II, III
    D. I, II, III

15. The speed of a reconstructed image is dependent on the

    A. reconstruction algorithm
    B. x-ray tube size
    C. detector type
    D. array processor

16. The two pieces of equipment that are located in the gantry of the CT scanner are the

    A. x-ray tube and filament
    B. x-ray tube and detectors
    C. filament and detectors
    D. digital-to-analog converter and filament

17. The _____ converts the x-ray photons into electrical signals (analog signal).

    A. analog-to-digital converter
    B. array processor

C. detector
D. digital-to-analog converter

18. The rows and columns in a grid characteristic are referred to as the

    A. voxel
    B. pixel
    C. matrix
    D. none of the above

19. A procedure done on the entire image in which the brightness of each pixel is measured is called

    A. scanning
    B. sampling
    C. quantization
    D. aliasing

20. The electrical signal strength is measured and a brightness value of each pixel is assigned a gray level.
    This is called

    A. sampling
    B. aliasing
    C. data acquisition
    D. quantization

21. The number of levels or shades of gray represented in the image is determined by

    A. the analog-to-digital converter
    B. sampling
    C. quantization
    D. all of the above

22. When the dimension of depth is added to the pixel, this is called a

    A. matrix
    B. slice thickness
    C. slice spacing
    D. voxel

23. Prepatient and postpatient collimators are used to

    A. minimize scatter radiation
    B. improve image contrast
    C. define slice thickness
    D. all of the above

24. The systematic collection of information from the patient to produce a CT image is called

    A. data acquisition
    B. image reconstruction
    C. image processing
    D. none of the above

25. When all the photons in a beam have the same energy, it is called a _____ beam.

    A. homogeneous
    B. polyenergetic
    C. heterogeneous
    D. none of the above

KEY (CORRECT ANSWERS)

1. C
2. B
3. B
4. B
5. A

6. A
7. B
8. B
9. A
10. C

11. B
12. B
13. A
14. A
15. D

16. B
17. C
18. C
19. B
20. D

21. D
22. D
23. D
24. A
25. A

TEST 3

DIRECTIONS: Each question or incomplete statement is followed by several suggested answers or completions. Select the one that BEST answers the question or completes the statement. *PRINT THE LETTER OF THE CORRECT ANSWER IN THE SPACE AT THE RIGHT.*

1. The quantity and quality of the photons change with the attenuation of a _____ beam. 1.____

    A. homogeneous
    B. monochromatic
    C. polychromatic
    D. all of the above

2. The relationship between the CT number and the variable shades of gray is referred to as 2.____

    A. filming
    B. windowing
    C. attenuation
    D. analog number

3. A 120 kVp technique is used in CT scanning because it 3.____
    I. reduces the dependency of attenuation coefficients on photon energy
    II. reduces the contrast between varying tissues
    III. produces a high radiation flux at the detectors
   The CORRECT answer is:

    A. I, II   B. I, III   C. II, III   D. I, II, III

4. The field of view in which transmission measurements are recorded during scanning is called _____ FOV. 4.____

    A. display
    B. reconstructed
    C. scan
    D. all of the above

5. Pixel size equals 5.____

    A. (slice thickness x matrix size) divided by field of view
    B. field of view divided by matrix size
    C. slice thickness x matrix x field of view
    D. display field of view divided by matrix size

6. Voxel size is determined by the 6.____

    A. slice thickness, matrix size, and exposure time
    B. field of view, matrix size, and scan field of view
    C. slice thickness, matrix, and field of view
    D. display field of view and matrix size

7. X-ray transmitted photons are measured by the 7.____

    A. analog-to-digital converter
    B. detectors
    C. digital-to-analog converter
    D. none of the above

8. The reference detector measures the radiation intensity

   A. from the x-ray tube
   B. transmitted through the patient
   C. after the postpatient collimator
   D. none of the above

9. Before the data can be sent to the computer, it must be converted into digital form. This process is done by the

   A. digital-to-analog converter
   B. analog-to-digital converter
   C. detectors
   D. host computer

10. The digital-to-analog converter is located between the
    I. image processor and the CRT display
    II. CRT display and film processor
    III. host computer and control terminal
    The CORRECT answer is:

    A. I, II   B. I, III   C. II, III   D. I, II, III

11. The components of the x-ray system in CT are the
    I. x-ray generator and x-ray tube
    II. x-ray beam filter and collimation
    III. x-ray tube, x-ray beam filter, and collimation
    The CORRECT answer is:

    A. I, II   B. I, III   C. II, III   D. I, II, III

12. The rotating anode x-ray tube disk is made of

    A. xenon, tungsten, and rhenium
    B. cesium fluoride, cesium iodide, and triode
    C. cesium fluoride, triode, and scintillation
    D. rhenium, tungsten, and molybdenum

13. _____ design is influenced by the size of the focal spot of the x-ray tube because of the penumbra effect.

    A. Postpatient collimation   B. Prepatient collimation
    C. Heat storage capacity   D. All of the above

14. A detector must exhibit several characteristics for CT image production. They are
    I. efficiency and response time
    II. dynamic range, high reproduceability, and stability
    III. efficiency, high reproduceability, and stability
    The CORRECT answer is:

    A. I, II   B. I, III   C. II, III   D. I, II, III

15. The data acquisition system (DAS) is the detector electronics that is positioned between the

    A. detector array and analog-to-digital converter
    B. analog-to-digital converter and host computer
    C. detector array and computer
    D. digital-to-analog converter and detector array

16. The MAJOR function of the DAS is

    A. measuring the transmitted x-ray beam
    B. measurements converted into binary code
    C. transmitting the digital data to the computer
    D. all of the above

17. The electrical signal from the detector is weak and must be amplified by the

    A. data acquisition system
    B. preamplifier
    C. detector array
    D. none of the above

18. The encoding device of the DAS is the

    A. analog-to-digital converter
    B. detector array
    C. array processor
    D. digital-to-analog converter

19. The _____ detectors convert x-ray energy directly into electrical energy.

    A. gas ionization
    B. scintillation
    C. xenon
    D. all of the above

20. The _____ detectors convert x-ray energy into light, then the light is converted into electrical energy.

    A. gas ionization
    B. scintillation
    C. xenon
    D. all of the above

21. The scintillation detectors use _____ to convert the light into electrical energy.

    A. scintillation crystals
    B. scintillation crystals and a photomultiplier tube
    C. a photomultiplier tube
    D. photodiodes

22. _____ detectors have excellent stability, fast response time, exhibit no after-glow problems, and their conversion efficiency is less then that of _____ detectors.

    A. Solid-state and xenon
    B. Scintillation and xenon
    C. Solid-state and scintillation
    D. Xenon and solid-state

23. The MAJOR systems in CT are

    A. imaging, computer and image display, recording, and storage
    B. imaging, computer, recording, and storage
    C. computer, image display, recording, and storage
    D. scanning, computer and image display

24. The _____ system receives the digital data from the DAS and processes it to reconstruct an image.

    A. scanning   B. display   C. imaging   D. computer

25. The computer system GENERALLY includes

    A. central processing units and array processors
    B. input-output, interface, and storage devices
    C. back-projector processor and communication hardware
    D. all of the above

KEY (CORRECT ANSWERS)

1. C
2. B
3. D
4. C
5. B

6. C
7. B
8. A
9. B
10. B

11. A
12. D
13. B
14. A
15. C

16. D
17. B
18. A
19. A
20. B

21. C
22. D
23. A
24. D
25. D

EXAMINATION SECTION
TEST 1

DIRECTIONS: Each question or incomplete statement is followed by several suggested answers or completions. Select the one that BEST answers the question or completes the statement. *PRINT THE LETTER OF THE CORRECT ANSWER IN THE SPACE AT THE RIGHT.*

1. The superior mediastinum is related to the anterior margins of thoracic vertebrae from _____ to _____.
   A. T1; T5   B. T2; T6   C. T1; T4   D. T2; T5

   1._____

2. The _____ is formed by the vertebral bodies anteriorly, the laminae and base of the spinous process posteriorly, and the pedicle laterally.
   A. neural foramina B. vertebral foramina
   C. spinal canal   D. osseous membrane

   2._____

3. A condition where the fifth lumbar vertebra may be partly or completely fused to the sacrum is called sacralization of
   A. L6   B. L5   C. L5-S2   D. none of the above

   3._____

Questions 4-15.
DIRECTIONS: Match the numbered cranial nerve pair in Questions 4 through 15 with the letter of its name in Column I.

COLUMN I
A. Vagus
B. Abducent
C. Hypoglossal
D. Facial
E. Motor oculi
F. Olfactory
G. Spinal accessory
H. Trochlear
I. Optic
J. Auditory
K. Trifacial
L. Glossopharyngeal
M. Parietal

4. First   4._____
5. Second   5._____
6. Third   6._____
7. Fourth   7._____
8. Fifth   8._____
9. Sixth   9._____
10. Seventh   10._____
11. Eighth   11._____
12. Ninth   12._____
13. Tenth   13._____
14. Eleventh   14._____
15. Twelfth   15._____

2 (#1)

Questions 16-30.

DIRECTIONS: Match the numbered definitions with the CORRECT lettered term from the following list.

16. Kyphosis

17. Nonmalignant growth containing vascular, fatty, and muscular tissues

18. Localized abnormal dilatation of a blood vessel, usually an artery. Due to the congenital defect of weakness of the wall of the vessel

19. Generalized pathology with disturbed normal architecture of the lobes due to infiltration of fibrous tissue and nodule formation

20. A condition where the vertebral disc pushes outward from its normal residence. Ruptures may occur anteriorly or posteriorly with a posterior rupture possibly pressing on the spinal cord

21. A sac or pouch in the walls of a canal or organ

22. Lordotic

23. The result of a rupture from a sclerosed or diseased blood vessel in the brain

24. Swelling and morbid changes in the lymph nodes; glandular disease

25. A chronic pulmonary disease characterized by the increase in the normal size of air spaces distal to the terminal bronchiole with destructive changes in their walls

26. A section of fat located upon the dura

27. A fibrous band holding parts together that are normally separated. This may involve the intestines or pericardial sac

28. A form of a tumor that is usually benign, consisting principally of blood vessels or lymph vessels

A. Adenopathy
B. Adhesion
C. Angiomyolipoma
D. Angioma
E. Aneurysm
F. Annulus
G. Cerebral hemorrhage
H. Cerebellum
I. Cirrhosis of the liver
J. Curvature of the cervical spine
K. Curvature of the thoracic spine
L. Disc herniation
J. Curvature of the cervical spine
K. Curvature of the thoracic spine
L. Disc herniation
M. Diverticulum
N. Emphysema
O. Epidural fat
P. Hemangioma

16.____
17.____
18.____
19.____
20.____
21.____
22.____
23.____
24.____
25.____
26.____
27.____
28.____

29. A ring-shaped structure that is related to the spinal discs and canals

30. Posterior portion of the brain lying dorsal to the pons and medulla oblongata, overhanging the latter

KEY (CORRECT ANSWERS)

1.	C	11.	J	21.	M		
2.	A	12.	L	22.	J		
3.	B	13.	A	23.	G		
4.	F	14.	G	24.	A		
5.	I	15.	C	25.	N		
6.	E	16.	K	26.	O		
7.	H	17.	C	27.	B		
8.	K	18.	E	28.	D		
9.	B	19.	I	29.	F		
10.	D	20.	L	30.	H		

TEST 2

Questions 1-5.

DIRECTIONS: Each question consists of a statement. You are to indicate whether the statement is TRUE (T) or FALSE (F).

1. Hemangiomas are the most commonly benign hepatic neoplasm with an autopsy incidence of about 4%. They are usually unifocal but multiple lesions are not infrequent. The tumors are classified into two types: cavernous hemangiomas which are small lesions usually less than 2 cm in diameter; and capillary hemangiomas which are large lesions ranging in size from 3-5 cm to almost completely replacing one or more hepatic lobes.   1.____

2. It is strongly felt that to properly identify hemangiomas on CT, it may be required to perform delayed scans of the liver at the area of the suspected lesions. This will help demonstrate peripheral enhancement followed by center enhancement equal to that of the surrounding tissues.   2.____

3. The pancreatic head lies between the superior mesentery vessels and the second portion of the duodenum.   3.____

4. The body of the pancreas lies posterior to the splenic vein.   4.____

5. Hemangiomas are composed of mature, thin-walled vessels of varying sizes having a capillary or cavernous pattern, or rarely an angiolipomatous pattern.   5.____

Questions 6-20.

DIRECTIONS: Match the numbered definition with the CORRECT lettered term from the following list.

6. Caused by prolapse of the nucleus pulposus into the endplate of the vertebra   6.____

7. A general term for growth of new tissue in the lymphatic system. Included in this general group are Hodgkin's disease, lymphatic leukemia, and reticuloses   7.____

8. Also known as the spinal canal, the foramina through which the spinal cord passes in the cervical, thoracic, and lumbar vertebrae   8.____

9. The death of a portion of tissue   9.____

10. Nipple-shaped process of the mastoid portion of the temporal bone extending downward and forward behind the external auditory meatus   10.____

A. Mastoid process
B. Pleura
C. Nerve root sleeve
D. Parenchyma
E. Stenosis
F. Lymphoma
G. Intrathecal contrast
H. Osteoporosis
I. Polyp
J. Spondylolisthesis
K. Necrosis
L. Schmorl's node
M. Hemangioma
N. Mucosal thickening
O. Cerebral sucus
P. Neural canal

2 (#2)

11. A furrow, groove, slight depression, or fissure in the brain. 11._____

12. Usually metriz iodinated contrast agent introduced into the subarachnoid space to visualize or demonstrate herniated discs, narrowed neural foramina, or occulted mass in the cord 12._____

13. Serous membrane that enfolds both lungs and is reflected upon the walls of the thorax and diaphragm 13._____

14. Usually regarding the gastrointestinal tract, especially related to the stomach and proximal small intestine 14._____

15. The sleeve through which the nerve passes through the spinal foramina 15._____

16. A benign tumor of a dilated blood vessel 16._____

17. The essential parts of an organ that are concerned with its function in contra-distinction to its framework 17._____

18. A disease process that results in the reduction of the bone per unit of volume 18._____

19. Forward subluxation of the lower lumbar vertebrae on the sacrum 19._____

20. Constriction or narrowing of a passage or orifice. Can be related to vessels, neural pathways, etc. 20._____

Questions 21-35.

DIRECTIONS: Match the numbered definition with the CORRECT lettered term from the following.

21. A condition where incomplete filling of contrast or attenuation of the x-ray beam does not take place

22. A benign bony tumor; a bone-like structure that develops on a bone, or occasionally, at other sites

A. Spur
B. Pericardial effusion
C. Hemangioma following an intravenous contrast injection
D. Pleural effusion
E. Polyp
F. Spina bifida

21._____

22._____

23. Inflammation of the lungs caused primarily by bacteria, viruses, and chemical irritants

24. A sharp or pointed projection. Often seen narrowing the neural canals

25. Blood in the urine

26. Fluid in the pericardial cavity, between the visceral and parietal pericardium

27. A condition where the mediastinum and its contents may be shifted laterally due to mass effect, enlargement of vessels, or enlargement of the lymph nodes

28. The lesions become isointense following administration of intravenous contrast

29. Hereditary condition marked by excessive calcification of bones causing spontaneous fractures and marble-like appearance

30. Fluid in the thoracic cavity between the visceral and parietal pleura

31. A swelling or mass of blood confined to an organ, tissue, or space which is caused by a break in a blood vessel

32. A tumor with a pedicle, commonly found in vascular organs such as the nose, uterus, and rectum

33. Degenerative arthritis or osteoarthritis of the cervical or lumbar vertebrae and related tissues. It may cause pressure on nerve roots with subsequent pain or paresthesia in the extremities

34. Congenital defect in the walls of the spinal canal caused by the lack of union between the laminae of the vertebrae. The section that is chiefly affected is the lumbar spine

35. Collection of urine in the renal pelvis due to obstructed outflow, forming a cyst by the production of distension and atrophy of organ

G. Stenosis
H. Osteoma
I. Hydronephrosis
J. Spondylosis
K. Hematuria
L. Hematoma
M. Osteopetrosis
N. Mediastinal shift
O. Partial opacification
P. Pneumonia

KEY (CORRECT ANSWERS)

1.	F	11.	O	21.	O	31.	L
2.	T	12.	G	22.	H	32.	E
3.	T	13.	B	23.	P	33.	J
4.	F	14.	N	24.	A	34.	F
5.	T	15.	C	25.	K	35.	I
6.	L	16.	M	26.	B		
7.	F	17.	D	27.	N		
8.	P	18.	H	28.	C		
9.	K	19.	J	29.	M		
10.	A	20.	E	30.	D		

TEST 3

Questions 1-12.

DIRECTIONS: For each of the following statements, indicate whether CT differentiation will be:
A. Cystic, or   B. Neoplastic
PRINT THE LETTER OF THE CORRECT ANSWER IN THE SPACE AT THE RIGHT.

1. If the margin of a renal mass is smooth   1.____

2. If the wall of a renal mass is thin with no measurable thickness   2.____

3. When the renal mass interfaces with the parenchyma and is demonstrated sharply and distinctly 3.____

4. When the renal mass interfaces with the parenchyma and is demonstrated indistinctly and irregularly 4.____

5. When the renal mass has an inhomogeneous density that is close to the renal parachyma plus 30 Hounsfield units 5.____

6. When the renal mass has a homogeneous density that is from a range of 0 to 50 Hounsfield units 6.____

7. When a renal mass demonstrates enhancement with the usage of an intravenous contrast agent 7.____

8. When a renal mass does not demonstrate enhancement with the usage of an intravenous contrast agent 8.____

9. When a renal mass demonstrates vascular invasion   9.____

10. If the shape of a renal mass is round and slightly oval   10.____

11. If the shape of a renal mass is irregular and lobulated   12.____

12. If the margin of a renal mass is lobulated   13.____

Questions 13-30.

DIRECTIONS: Each question consists of a statement. You are to indicate whether the statement is TRUE (T) or FALSE (F). *PRINT THE LETTER OF THE CORRECT ANSWER IN THE SPACE AT THE RIGHT.*

13. One indication of metastasis in the liver following intravenous iodine injection is non-enhancing lesions while the rest of the liver enhances. However, there are indications that liver lesions will enhance at the same level as the rest of the liver. 13.____

14. There is a constant relationship between the non-enhanced liver and the   14.____
    non-enhanced spleen. Therefore, the liver averages 8 Hounsfield units greater
    than the spleen and does not measure less than the spleen. Fatty infiltration
    results in the liver having an attenuation less than the spleen on a non-contrast
    CT. Bolus or post-intravenous injection of contrast is unreliable to compare the
    Hounsfield units because the liver and the spleen may enhance at different
    times.

15. A majority of the lesions of a fatty infiltration are in the 0 to 30 Hounsfield   15.____
    range resulting in a significant overlap with primary and metastatic neoplasms.
    There are diffuse fatty infiltrates that may obscure dilated biliary ducts or low
    attenuation lesions within the liver.

16. An aortic aneurysm measuring over 5 cm in AP diameter is a critical concern   16.____
    as well as an immediate indication for surgery.

17. At the level of the kidneys, the aorta tends to normally lie midline of the body. 17.____
    Therefore, the inferior vena cava tends to lie to the left.

18. A stomach which is filled with oral contrast and partially digested food may   18.____
    give a false indication of gastric lymphoma, gastric adenocarcinoma, or gastric
    carcinoma.

19. A -100 Hounsfield units is equivalent to the CT density of the retroperitoneal   19.____
    and perigastric fatty tissue.

20. The body of the pancreas lies between the right kidney and the body of the   20.____
    stomach, with the pancreatic head curving to the right side of the aorta.

21. The central cavity or body of the lateral ventricle is situated in the middle of 21.____
    the parietal lobe.

22. A contrasted spleen is a good measuring point for liver comparison.   22.____

23. The azygamous vein is located in the upper thorax of either lung.   23.____

24. One cause of stroke or TIA can be a reduction of the internal caliber of   24.____
    the carotid artery.

25. Nasal polyps can ONLY be visualized in the coronal plane when scanning   25.____
    the sinuses.

26. A non-contrasted spleen is a good measuring point for liver comparison.   26.____

27. The two parts that make up the intervertebral discs are the central   27.____
    nucleus pulposus and the peripheral annulus fibrosus.

28. The lumbar discs are thicker anteriorly, a feature which contributes to the   28.____
    normal lumbar kyphosis.

29. Slightly inferior to the thoracic inlet at the level of T-3, the esophagus is posterior to the trachea.   29._____

30. The submaxillary gland is located below the tongue.   30._____

KEY (CORRECT ANSWERS)

1.	A	11.	B	21.	T
2.	A	12.	B	22.	F
3.	A	13.	T	23.	F
4.	B	14.	T	24.	T
5.	B	15.	T	25.	T
6.	A	16.	T	26.	T
7.	B	17.	F	27.	T
8.	A	18.	T	28.	F
9.	B	19.	T	29.	T
10.	A	20.	F	30.	F

TEST 4

DIRECTIONS: Each question consists of a statement. You are to indicate whether the statement is TRUE (T) or FALSE (F). *PRINT THE LETTER OF THE CORRECT ANSWER IN THE SPACE AT THE RIGHT.*

1. The classic characteristics of a non-simple cyst are mural nodularity, wall thickening, and a fluid-filled level. 1.____

2. Although post-contrast CT enhancement of the liver is excellent for delineating some masses and carcinoma, a pre-intravenous contrast CT of the liver does highlight and indicate some non-visualized metastasis. 2.____

3. An indication of carcinoma on a post-intravenous contrast CT of the liver is a ring or peripheral enhancement with an additional enhancement of the center. 3.____

4. The partial volume effect can cause a high attenuation value. 4.____

5. A CT examination is a good test to demonstrate renal function. 5.____

6. A CT examination will demonstrate renal function in regards to blunt trauma. 6.____

7. Atelectasis is a collapsed or airless condition of the lung. 7.____

8. Bronchiolectasis is the dilatation of the capillaries. 8.____

9. A characteristic of cysts in the liver on post-intravenous contrast CT is edge enhancement without the center enhancing. 9.____

10. The left bronchus is longer and more vertical than the right bronchus. 10.____

11. The anterior surface of the sacrum is concave. 11.____

12. In the female, the prostate gland controls the flow of urine from the urinary bladder to the urethra. 12.____

13. Another name for the hyoid bone is the lingual bone. 13.____

14. The posterior mediastinum is bound laterally by the lungs, anteriorly and superiorly by the tracheal bifurcation, inferiorly by the pericardium, and posteriorly by the thoracic spine. 14.____

15. The hepatic and splenic arteries branch off of the aorta at nearly the same level. The renal arteries are inferior, and are located below the superior mesenteric artery. However, the inferior mesenteric artery is located inferior to the renal arteries. 15.____

16. The sacrum may contain what is called disc remnants. They may be at S1-2 and S2-3.   16.____

17. When performing an IAC study that acquires a cholesteatoma, this information is BEST demonstrated with coronal reformations from thin axial slices.   17.____

18. The diaphragm is a muscular membranous wall separating the abdomen from the thoracic cavity with its convexity upwards.   18.____

19. It is a typical finding that, as the bronchi extend distally from the main bronchus, the caliber of the bronchi decreases.   19.____

20. Breast implants cannot be visualized on a CT examination.   20.____

21. It is easier to detect disc protrusions or neural foramina damage with the use of sagittal reformations that are created from axial scans of the spine.   21.____

22. Due to the inability to sometimes visualize disc protrusions on CT, it has been necessary to introduce contrast into the spinal canal and then perform post-contrast CT slices through the area of interest.   22.____

23. At the level of the manubrium and the first rib, the esophagus is located anterior to the trachea.   23.____

24. The thyroid gland is a non-paired gland.   24.____

25. The parathyroid gland is a paired gland.   25.____

26. Osteosarcoma or other types of bone carcinoma cannot be visualized on CT.   26.____

27. The right lobe of the liver is larger than the left lobe.   27.____

28. Adrenal glands can be visualized on just about every CT scan. Non-visualization is an indication that there may be problems.   28.____

29. The classic characteristics of a simple cyst are that they are homogenous, with a sharp zone of transition with normal parenchyma, and they have the same attenuation value as water.   29.____

30. There is a difference in the number of lobes between the right and left lungs because of the heart.   30.____

KEY (CORRECT ANSWERS)

1.	T	11.	T	21.	T
2.	T	12.	F	22.	T
3.	F	13.	T	23.	F
4.	T	14.	T	24.	F
5.	T	15.	T	25.	F
6.	T	16.	T	26.	F
7.	T	17.	T	27.	T
8.	F	18.	T	28.	F
9.	F	19.	T	29.	T
10.	T	20.	F	30.	T

MUSCULOSKELETAL SYSTEM & INJURIES
EXAMINATION SECTION
TEST 1

DIRECTIONS: Each question or incomplete statement is followed by several suggested answers or completions. Select the one that BEST answers the question or completes the statement. *PRINT THE LETTER OF THE CORRECT ANSWER IN THE SPACE AT THE RIGHT.*

1. All of the following are part of the musculoskeletal system EXCEPT

   A. bones and muscles
   B. ligaments and tendons
   C. spleen and liver
   D. cartilage

   1.___

2. The musculoskeletal system is NOT responsible for

   A. support and shape
   B. clearance of waste products
   C. protection and locomotion
   D. production of red blood cells

   2.___

3. The spinal column performs all of the following functions EXCEPT

   A. protect the spinal cord
   B. support the head and trunk
   C. carry impulses from the brain to the other parts of the body
   D. more than one but not all of the above

   3.___

4. All of the following correlations of rate, area, and cause of incidence are true regarding spinal column injury EXCEPT:

   A. low; cervical and lumbar spine; good support
   B. high; cervical and lumbar spine; lack of support
   C. low; thoracic spine; support of the ribs
   D. low; sacrum; support of the pelvis

   4.___

5. Regarding the rib cage, it is NOT true that the

   A. upper seven pairs of ribs are joined in front by the sternum
   B. next three pairs of ribs are joined by cartilage attached to the sternum
   C. eleventh and twelfth pairs of ribs have no front attachment
   D. clavicle or collarbone does not support the sternum

   5.___

6. Major components of joints include all of the following EXCEPT

   A. bone ends covered with articular cartilage
   B. synovial membrane which produces a lubricating fluid
   C. capsules in a thin elastic layer
   D. ligaments or bands of connective tissue that bind the bones together, allowing some flexibility

   6.___

7. Ball and socket joints provide a range of motion which is

   A. restricted to the left side only of the joint
   B. restricted only to the right side of the joint
   C. wide in all directions
   D. all of the above

8. Pelvis hip bones consist of all of the following EXCEPT the

   A. ileum   B. carpals   C. ischium   D. pubis

9. The functions of skeletal muscles do NOT include

   A. only exerting force by contracting
   B. working in pairs
   C. not moving the bones
   D. tendons attaching the muscles to the bones

10. Among the different types of muscles in the body is (are) _____ muscles.

    A. voluntary
    C. cardiac
    B. involuntary
    D. all of the above

11. When a bone is broken at the point of impact, it is called a

    A. twisting injury
    C. fatigue fracture
    B. direct injury
    D. none of the above

12. A fracture occurring at some distance from the impact is referred to as a(n)

    A. pathologic fracture
    C. indirect injury
    B. direct injury
    D. twisting injury

13. Joints, such as those between the bones of the hand, which allow very subtle and delicate movement are called _____ joints.

    A. ball and socket
    C. pivot
    B. gliding
    D. all of the above

14. Joints, such as those of the fingers, which permit flexion and extension are called _____ joints.

    A. hinge
    C. gliding
    B. pivot
    D. ball and socket

15. The _____ is a bone covered by a membrane.

    A. synovial membrane
    C. periosteum
    B. pericardium
    D. all of the above

16. The strength and hardness of bone is due PRIMARILY to

    A. calcium
    C. phosphorus
    B. sodium
    D. A and C *only*

17. Smooth or involuntary muscle mostly constitutes the muscle of the internal organs. Such muscle can be found in the walls of the

    A. urinary bladder
    B. blood vessels
    C. digestive system
    D. all of the above

17.____

18. Muscle contraction requires energy, which is derived from the metabolism of glucose and results in the production of

    A. galactose
    B. lactic acid
    C. lactose
    D. none of the above

18.____

19. Of the following injuries, which one MOST frequently occurs in association with pelvic fracture?

    A. Urinary bladder injury
    B. Femoral head dislocation
    C. Popliteal artery rupture
    D. None of the above

19.____

20. The fracture which occurs in children whose bones are still pliable, is a break straight across the bone, and goes only part-way through the bone is called _____ fracture.

    A. spiral
    B. greenstick
    C. impacted
    D. comminuted

20.____

21. The injuries in which ligaments are partially torn, usually as a result of the sudden twisting of a joint beyond its normal range of motion, are

    A. strains
    B. sprains
    C. dislocations
    D. none of the above

21.____

22. Soft tissue injuries or muscle spasms around a joint characterized by pain on active movement are called

    A. strains
    B. sprains
    C. dislocations
    D. A and B *only*

22.____

23. The pre-hospital management of a victim with anterior dislocation of the sternoclavicular joint would MOST likely include a(n)

    A. cold pack sling
    B. air splint
    C. pad axilla
    D. none of the above

23.____

24. A victim who sustained a clavicle fracture as a result of a direct blow would MOST likely receive the pre-hospital treatment of a(n)

    A. cold pack sling and swath
    B. air splint
    C. board splint
    D. none of the above

24.____

Questions 25-30.

DIRECTIONS: In Questions 25 through 30, match the numbered description with the lettered classification of fracture, listed in the column below, which it BEST describes. Place the letter of the CORRECT answer in the appropriate space at the right.

CLASSIFICATION OF FRACTURES
A. Transverse
B. Spiral
C. Impacted
D. Comminuted
E. Oblique
F. Greenstick

25. Ends of broken bones are jammed into each other.   25.____
26. Break forms an angle to the shaft.   26.____
27. Break is straight across the shaft of a bone.   27.____
28. Bone is fragmented.   28.____
29. Fracture has the appearance of a spring; break twists around the shaft of the bone.   29.____
30. Fracture is incomplete and common in children whose bones are still soft and pliable.   30.____

KEY (CORRECT ANSWERS)

1.	C	16.	D
2.	B	17.	D
3.	C	18.	B
4.	A	19.	A
5.	D	20.	B
6.	C	21.	B
7.	C	22.	A
8.	B	23.	D
9.	C	24.	C
10.	D	25.	C
11.	B	26.	E
12.	C	27.	A
13.	B	28.	D
14.	A	29.	B
15.	C	30.	F

TEST 2

DIRECTIONS: Each question or incomplete statement is followed by several suggested answers or completions. Select the one that BEST answers the question or completes the statement. *PRINT THE LETTER OF THE CORRECT ANSWER IN THE SPACE AT THE RIGHT.*

1. To immobilize a fracture of the _____, use a _____.   1._____

   A. hip; full backboard
   B. foot or ankle; pillow
   C. shoulder or clavicle; sling or swathe
   D. all of the above

2. The MAJOR complication of anterior dislocation of the shoulder is _____ injury.   2._____

   A. radial damage
   B. axillary nerve
   C. subclavian artery
   D. all of the above

3. Possible complications of posterior dislocation of the sternoclavicular joint include   3._____

   A. damage to trachea
   B. damage to esophagus
   C. pneumothorax
   D. all of the above

4. One possible complication of a clavicular fracture may be   4._____

   A. subclavian artery injury
   B. axillary artery injury
   C. Volk-Mannis ischemic contracture
   D. none of the above

5. A victim involved in a motor vehicle accident sustained a fracture of the shaft of the humerus. He has ecchymosis, swelling and deformity of the area. Among the complications he may encounter is _____ nerve injury.   5._____

   A. ulner
   B. radial
   C. median
   D. all of the above

6. Pre-hospital treatment of a fracture of the shaft of the humerus includes   6._____

   A. sling and swathe
   B. padded board splint
   C. hot pack
   D. A and B *only*

7. The MOST likely complication of an elbow fracture (e.g., skateboard injury) is   7._____

   A. Volk-Mannis ischemic contracture
   B. chook
   C. wrist drop
   D. A and C *only*

8. A victim who falls on a hyperextended arm and develops locked painful elbow is MOST likely to develop which of the following complications?   8._____

   A. Ulner nerve injury
   B. Vascular injury
   C. Associated injuries to the rib
   D. All of the above

9. Pre-hospital management of a forearm fracture would include

 A. air splint
 B. padded board splint
 C. all of the above
 D. none of the above

10. The signs and symptoms of dislocation include

 A. an obvious deformity of the joint
 B. swelling at the joint and pain which increases with movement
 C. loss of use of the joint or complaint of a locked or frozen joint
 D. all of the above

11. The MOST common symptom of strain is

 A. pain
 B. discoloration
 C. hematoma
 D. all of the above

12. Among the common symptoms of a sprain is

 A. swelling
 B. discoloration
 C. pain on movement
 D. all of the above

13. Of the following, the FIRST priority of care is for fractures of the

 A. spine
 B. head, rib cage, and pelvis
 C. extremities
 D. none of the above

14. When a bone is broken or dislocated, the process of _____ supplies a substitute support and immobilization to the bone.

 A. traction
 B. splinting
 C. all of the above
 D. none of the above

15. A _____ fracture is the fracture of the wrist that gives a silverfork appearance.

 A. boxer's
 B. colles
 C. nightstick
 D. none of the above

16. A garden spade deformity occurs when a victim

 A. falls on his outstretched hand
 B. falls on his extended wrist
 C. gets his hand slammed in a car door
 D. all of the above

17. General treatment of injuries to the lower extremities includes

 A. pulse and nerve function assessment
 B. manual traction
 C. spinal protection
 D. all of the above

3 (#2)

Questions 18-19.

DIRECTIONS: Questions 18 and 19 are to be answered on the basis of the following information.
A victim is hit by a car and suffers hematoma of the scrotum. He is complaining of pain on compression of the iliac wings. You suspect a pelvic fracture.

18. Pre-hospital treatment, after the ABCs, may include 18.____

   A. mast
   B. backboard
   C. IV fluid
   D. all of the above

19. Among the possible complications of the above patient's condition is 19.____

   A. shock
   B. bladder or urethra injury
   C. associated spinal injury
   D. all of the above

20. A victim who has a dislocated knee may also have 20.____

   A. shock
   B. sciatic nerve injury
   C. popliteal artery injury
   D. all of the above

21. A victim who sustained an angulated tibia and fibula fracture is at high risk of developing 21.____

   A. shock
   B. compartment syndrome
   C. an associated lumbar spine fracture
   D. all of the above

22. All of the following sets of bones are part of the hand EXCEPT 22.____

   A. carpals
   B. metatarsals
   C. metacarpals
   D. phalanges

23. A fracture of the fifth metacarpal MOST typically occurs in 23.____

   A. boxers
   B. duelers
   C. wrestlers
   D. none of the above

24. The proximal bony projection of the ulna at the elbow which constitutes the *funny bone* is called the 24.____

   A. olecranon
   B. patella
   C. humerus
   D. malleolus

25. The tough bands of tissue connecting bone to bone around a joint or supporting internal organs within the body are called 25.____

   A. synovial joints
   B. ligaments
   C. tendons
   D. malleolus

Questions 26-30.

DIRECTIONS: In Questions 26 through 30, match the numbered description with the lettered part of the musculoskeletal system, listed in Column I, which it BEST describes. Place the letter of the CORRECT answer in the appropriate space at the right.

COLUMN I
A. Axial skeleton
B. Appendicular skeleton
C. Tendon
D. Tibia
E. Trochanter

26. The part of the skeleton comprising the upper and lower extremities 26.___

27. The part of the skeleton comprising the skull, spinal column and rib cage 27.___

28. Either of the two processes below the neck of the femur 28.___

29. The fibrous portion of muscle that attaches to bone 29.___

30. The shin bone 30.___

Questions 31-35.

DIRECTIONS: In Questions 31 through 35, match the numbered description with the lettered part of the musculoskeletal system, listed in Column I, which it BEST describes. Place the letter of the CORRECT answer in the appropriate space at the right.

COLUMN I
A. Diaphysis
B. Epiphysis
C. Periosteum
D. Acetabulum
E. Metatarsals

31. Strong, white, fibrous material which covers the bone 31.___

32. Portion of spongy bone covered with compact bone 32.___

33. Central shaft of a long bone composed of compact bone 33.___

34. Foot bones 34.___

35. Cup-shaped cavity in which the rounded head of the femur rotates 35.___

KEY (CORRECT ANSWERS)

1.	D	16.	B
2.	B	17.	D
3.	D	18.	D
4.	A	19.	D
5.	B	20.	C
6.	D	21.	B
7.	A	22.	B
8.	B	23.	A
9.	C	24.	A
10.	D	25.	B
11.	A	26.	B
12.	D	27.	A
13.	A	28.	E
14.	B	29.	C
15.	B	30.	D

31. C
32. B
33. A
34. E
35. D

BASIC FUNDAMENTALS OF X-RAY EXAMINATIONS

CONTENTS

		Page
I.	BASIC PRINCIPLES	1
II.	BASIC INFORMATION	1
	A. Why be Concerned about Radiation Exposure Generally	2
	B. When to be Especially Concerned	2
III.	BASIC PRACTICES	5
	A. Emphasis on Quality	6
	B. Choice of Equipment	6
	C. Installation	6
	D. Filters	6
	E. Beam Restrictors	6
	F. Gonadal Shields	7
	G. Films and Screens	7
	H. Film Processing	8
	I. Techniques for Examinations	8
	J. Interpretation	8

BASIC FUNDAMENTALS OF X-RAY EXAMINATIONS

I. BASIC PRINCIPLES

Recent investigations of x-ray use in the United States showed that approximately 60 percent of all diagnostic radiologic studies are now supervised by radiologists; however, almost all physicians are involved in making decisions to perform radiological examinations. This guide emphasizes the considerations necessary in deciding to perform an x-ray examination; it also reviews principles of good practice in the use of x-ray equipment. These considerations and principles do not interfere with the prerogative of the physician but they do require his cooperation if optimal good for the individual patient and for public health are to be achieved.

The basic principles may be summarized as follows:

1. In almost every medical situation, when a physician feels there is a reasonable expectation of obtaining information from a radiological examination that would affect the medical care of an individual, potential radiation hazard is not a consideration.

2. In diagnostic radiology, the goal is to obtain the desired information -- using the smallest radiation exposure that is practical.

3. Emphasis should be given to the technical means (collimators, filters, gonadal shielding, and so forth) by which radiation dose can be reduced without impairment of the medical value of the procedure.

4. Each physician should give due consideration to the potential somatic consequences of radiation exposure to the patient, and to the genetic effects upon mankind, as part of his responsibility toward public health.

5. The physician should retain complete freedom of judgment in the selection of radiographic procedures, and he should conform with good technical practice.

Equipment manufacturers, radiation safety experts and inspectors, technologists and others make important contributions to the efficient use of radiation in medical diagnosis, but the ultimate responsibility rests with the attending and consulting physicians. This guide is intended to aid physicians in exercising appropriate judgment.

II. BASIC INFORMATION

X-ray examinations are important in the diagnosis of most patients with serious illness or the potentiality of such illness. They have been of proven importance in preventive medical programs such as mass chest surveys and probably have a place in periodic health examinations.

Even if the examination is actually performed by a specialist in radiology, the attending physician usually decides when to refer individual patients for diagnostic x-ray procedures. His clinical judgment largely determines their frequency and influences the kinds of procedures and their comprehensiveness.

This part is designed:

To provide the attending physician with basic information concerning the factors involved in x-ray diagnosis of his own patients.

To provide information that every physician should have as part of his responsibility to public health -- particularly in reference to *third party* situations such as mass x-ray survey programs and pre-employment radiological examinations.

Two broad considerations are involved: why human radiation exposure is important generally, and specific situations in which there is need to be especially concerned.

A. *WHY BE CONCERNED ABOUT RADIATION EXPOSURE GENERALLY?*

   1. Possible genetic effects

   Sound theoretical considerations suggest that even small amounts of radiation exposure to the gonads can adversely affect the genetic inheritance of future generations. This has led to the widely accepted principle that no amount of gonadal exposure is as small as to be dismissed as harmless.

   2. Possible effects on the patient

   Although no significant somatic change has been demonstrated in adults as a result of the low doses incurred in diagnostic radiology, there is laboratory evidence that even less levels of radiation may affect some cells; however, several epidemiological studies suggest that special consideration must be given to the relatively high radio sensitivity of the fetus in utero, particularly during the early phases of gestation.

   3. Increasing need -- increasing use

   The increased personnel and social resources available in recent years for health care, together with improvement in the versatility and precision of diagnostic radiology, have brought a steady increase in x-ray examinations -- amounting to an increment of about 7 percent annually. This trend is likely to continue. Naturally, there has been and will be a corresponding potential for more radiation exposure.

B. *WHEN TO BE ESPECIALLY CONCERNED*

In almost every medical situation, when a physician feels there is a reasonable expectation that radiological examination will benefit the health of an individual, radiation hazard is not a contraindication.

The principle applies even in the case of pregnant women. The amount of previous medical radiation exposure to the nonpregnant patient is not relevant in deciding whether a procedure should be performed.

In each case, the physician may judge whether there is a reasonable expectation of useful information from a proposed examination. In making that judgment, he must take into account the theoretical risk involved. Consultation with the radiologist on the medical problem of a specific patient often leads to selection of the most appropriate procedure and also minimizes unproductive exposure. Examinations can sometimes be abbreviated without loss of diagnostic information. The potential hazard, however small, varies with the age of the patient and the part of the body being examined. Particular categories of individuals also require special consideration. Examples are given below.

1. The parents of future generations

    (a) Young Males

    A recent national x-ray survey by the United States Public Health Service included a study of genetically significant doses of radiation received by the United States population. The data showed that the largest contribution is from examination of males in the 15 to 29 age group. Most of this dose is received from studies of the abdominal and pelvic regions, where the gonads may be included in the primary beam. Examinations of these regions in young males should be performed only when there is clear clinical need. Optimal technical conditions are required, including beam area restriction and gonadal shielding whenever it does not interfere with the examination. For any complex symptoms involving these areas, it is often advisable to perform an initial study and evaluate the information obtained rather than to request three or four procedures simultaneously. Consultation with the radiologist is valuable here.

    (b) Young Females

    The same considerations apply to potentially procreative females as to males since the genetic consequences of radiation are comparable. Practically, however, gonadal shielding is far more difficult to achieve for females without seriously compromising the examination. On the other hand, the natural shielding of the ovaries by overlying tissues result in a substantially smaller gonadal dose for females than for males for several types of lower abdominal area examinations. Closer attention to beam area restriction and specific gonadal shielding is nevertheless highly desirable.

    (c) Pregnant Women (and Women Who Might Be Pregnant)

    The concern here is with the unborn child. X-ray procedures that include the uterus of women who are, or who might be, pregnant require particular guidelines in selection and timing. Examinations of other parts of the body maybe done at any time provided such examinations are conducted under conditions limiting the radiation exposure to the amount necessary for adequate examination.

    In all women of childbearing age who may be pregnant, the period of choice for examinations involving the abdomen and pelvis is the first 14 days after onset of a menstrual period. In the remainder of the menstrual cycle of women who may be pregnant, the physician should consider whether he would still ask for the examination if the woman were known to be pregnant.

    If the physician considers the examination necessary for immediate patient care, it should be conducted in accordance with good technical practice, even if the patient is pregnant. If he considers the examination useful but not necessary for immediate care, he should consider postponing it.

    In the event that an examination is postponed because of the possibility of pregnancy, and the woman does prove to be pregnant, then a new decision is necessary as to whether further postponement is allowable. This situation is responsible for the recommendation that the ONLY examinations which should be considered for postponement are those which could be further postponed until at least the latter half of pregnancy, without seriously compromising the proper medical care of the patient. The reason for such further postponement, if possible, is that the relatively higher radio sensitivity of the fetus is greater during the first trimester as compared to a later trimester of prenatal life.

(d) A Practical Policy for X-ray Examinations of Pregnant Women

The need for an x-ray examination of abdomen and pelvis varies in its importance for the patient's benefit, and the physician must apply a broad scale of urgency, not susceptible to precise definition. At one extreme would be the example of a patient thought to be pregnant and who had relatively minor gastrointestinal or urinary tract symptoms of the type that frequently occur during pregnancy. In this case, there probably is not sufficient indication for a gastrointestinal examination or an excretory urogram. If, on the other hand, the patient has unexplained hematuria or melena, there would be adequate indication for proceeding with such a study, even in the case of confirmed pregnancy in the first trimester. In such circumstances, the radiologist should be informed of the pregnancy so that, if possible, the examination could be modified to reduce the radiation dose to a level even lower than usual.

If an x-ray examination is performed before the patient's pregnancy is discovered, there is normally little cause for concern. In most procedures, the radiation exposure is so small that the risk of interference with fetal development is negligible. Such radiation exposure alone should not be used as a justification for interruption of the pregnancy. In very unusual circumstances when it is suspected that a diagnostic procedure or combination of procedures may have resulted in an uncommonly large exposure, efforts should be made to determine the fetal dose and experts should be consulted about the possible hazard.

2. Group and survey studies

(a) Survey Programs

Many physicians are asked to advise public agencies or other organizations interested in health surveyor screening programs. Such survey programs which involve radiographic examinations of healthy persons should be assessed for productivity. Only those programs that result in significant case finding are defensible. Most survey programs employ photofluorography of the chest. The main target is tuberculosis, which has not been completely overcome as a health problem in the United States.

Such activities must be justified in terms of detecting previously undiagnosed and unsuspected cases of active tuberculosis and thus, in most instances, should be limited to areas of high population density and low economic status where the incidence is greatest. Health authorities have suggested two or three cases or more per 10,000 examinations as a reasonable yield in terms of health benefits gained as opposed to the risk associated with subjecting large numbers of people to radiation exposure, small though that exposure may be to each individual.

Furthermore, real benefit from the programs, even those that attain high productivity in case finding is contingent upon effective follow-up of positive findings.

(b) Children's Chests

As an initial screening procedure for tuberculosis in infants and children, the tuberculin test is preferable to large-scale x-ray survey programs. Subsequent chest x-ray examinations are usually indicated only for positive findings.

(c) Mother's Chests

Prenatal survey programs are worthwhile where the incidence of tuberculosis may be relatively high because of socioeconomic or other factors. This is particularly so because undetected tuberculosis is especially hazardous for pregnant women. Properly done radiographs, and even photofluorograms, involve such minute doses that they represent an acceptable hazard for the fetus when there is expectation of a high yield of active tuberculosis.

(d) Hospital Admissions

Justification for performing chest x-ray examinations of all persons admitted to a hospital also depends on the yield of cases of tuberculosis. In turn, yield may depend upon the kind of hospital or service and the socioeconomic characteristics of the population the institution serves. If such programs are undertaken, they should include mechanisms for rapid interpretation, prompt follow-up of positive findings, and periodic reappraisal of productivity. The yield is always the primary factor. It tends to be higher from hospital admissions than from community surveys.

(e) Medical and Paramedical Personnel

This group is at high risk for tuberculosis. In most hospitals and clinics, the case yield will be such as to justify periodic chest x-ray examinations of personnel dealing directly with patients.

(f) Service Groups

In view of the potential tuberculosis hazard to the community, groups such as food handlers, barbers, beauticians, teachers, and others rendering personal service should have a chest film at least annually.

(g) Periodic Health Examinations

Health authorities are not in agreement on the value of periodic health examinations as a whole or on the value of chest x-rays in such programs. The radiation hazard of a chest radiograph obtained with good technique is minute with an estimated mean annual genetically significant dose contribution of 0.7 mrad.

(h) Special Occupational Groups

Periodic chest x-ray examinations are recommended for persons engaged in occupations with special pulmonary disease hazards such as miners and workers who have contact with beryllium, asbestos, glass, silica, and so forth. The premise that discovery of these special occupational illnesses in the recognizable but still asymptomatic phase has a beneficial effect upon the outcome is now generally accepted.

(I) Pre-employment Lumbar Spine Examinations

With this type of procedure, selected groups of healthy people are exposed to pelvic irradiation without clear-cut clinical indications. Protection of the public at large is less significant than in tuberculosis surveys. The practice cannot be categorically condemned, however, since it is based on a desire to obtain evidence of the likelihood of aggravating a pre-existing condition. It is not yet established whether the yield, in terms of prevention of injury, justifies the procedures. The gonadal region is involved, and the subjects are mainly young males. Since there is no urgency in the procedure, the very best technique can always be used in performing the examinations. Gonadal shielding should always be used.

III. BASIC PRACTICES

X-ray usage for most physicians and technicians should involve only radiography. Unless he has had special training in fluoroscopy, the nonradiologist should not use this procedure. Fluoroscopic examination has advantages only, when the dynamics of the body are to be studied. Fluoroscopy involves much greater radiation exposure than radiography. Considerable special training is required to do it well and with minimal radiation exposure. In no circumstances should fluoroscopy be used as a substitute for a procedure in which radiography is clearly indicated.

Guidelines to good radiography include:

A. *EMPHASIS ON QUALITY*

The value of a radiographic examination is directly related to the quality of the radiograph produced. Many of the technical factors that combine to produce good radiographs also tend to minimize radiation exposure. Good technique also reduces exposure by reducing the number of radiographs that must be repeated.

If a nonradiologist decides to undertake x-ray examinations, he should prepare himself properly. He should obtain equipment suitable and adequate for the types of examinations he plans to perform. He may delegate some aspects of the examination to an assistant, but the responsibility for quality control cannot be delegated. The physician himself must make sure that examinations are done properly and without unnecessary exposure. He should attain and maintain through postgraduate education, competence to interpret the radiographs.

B. *CHOICE OF EQUIPMENT*

Planning the installation involves the purchase of equipment and the design of an adequate radiographic room and darkroom. The selection of an x-ray machine appropriate for the proposed examinations can be made by consultation with radiologists and radiological physicists and also by reference to various resource publications.

C. *INSTALLATION*

The installation of an x-ray unit is usually apart of the sales contract. During the course of such installation, it is generally necessary to provide shielding for walls, floors, and ceilings against which the x-ray beam might be directed. The required degree of protection can be derived from various resource materials. In most instances, the physician will want to consult a suitable expert, usually a radiological physicist, to help with selection of equipment, planning of protection factors, and inspection and calibration of the equipment after installation. The physicist can also advise on the establishment of a film badge or other personnel monitoring system as a continuing check of the radiation protection measures and practices of the physician and technologist.

In some states, there will also be pertinent regulations and inspections. The physician should familiarize himself with these at an early stage of planning.

D. *FILTERS*

Even at high kilo voltage settings used in modern radiographic techniques, the x-ray beam always contains, some rays of low penetrating power that have no value in medical examinations. These add to the patient's absorbed dose without contributing to the diagnostic information. A large proportion of these useless rays are filtered out of the beam if the tube aperture is covered with at least 2 millimeters of aluminum or equivalent. Although most modern machines are equipped with such filters, this should not be assumed. The type of filter provided by the manufacturer or vendor should be clearly stated at the time of purchase. If a removable filter is provided, it is important to make sure that the filter is in place each time the machine is used.

E. *BEAM RESTRICTORS*

Only that part of the x-ray beam that falls on the film can provide useful information. The rest contributes nothing to diagnostic information, but adds unnecessarily to the patient's radiation dose and may contribute to the unintended exposure of other persons in the vicinity. Failure to limit the beam area properly is one of the most frequent causes of unnecessary radiation exposure.

Most x-ray machines can be purchased or equipped with adjustable collimating devices that can be used to restrict the size and shape of the x-ray beam. It is usually best for collimators to be equipped with a light localizer, which provides a visual indication of size and location of the radiation beam at any distance. The machine operator must adjust the opening of the collimator, for each examination performed, to the dimensions appropriate to the area being examined. Automated collimators are expected to be standard equipment on all machines produced beginning in 1972.

Before development of the adjustable collimator, the standard method of restricting the beam area was to place a non-adjustable cone or diaphragm over the aperture of the x-ray tube. Several cones or diaphragms were usually needed to allow for different film sizes. This method can still be used if varied sizes are provided and if the operator is conscientious in using the cone or diaphragm appropriate for the examination and the film size. Test radiographs should be made after installation to determine the effectiveness of collimating devices.

All these devices have an important function in addition to limiting patient dose. They improve the contrast and detail of the radiographic image by reducing the amount of scattered radiation reaching the film. If two radiographs are made under identical conditions, except that one is done with collimation and the other without, the one with collimation will show a decided superiority in image quality.

F. *GONADAL SHIELDS*

Suitable protective devices (usually lead) should be provided to shield the gonads of patients who are potentially procreative when the gonads cannot be excluded from the beam by collimation. Gonadal shields are not used when their presence would obscure important areas or otherwise interfere with the examination.

The use of special shields for the gonads during diagnostic radiology is still a developing art, and equipment for this purpose has not become standardized. The testes can usually be covered by some radiation barrier material with ease. In addition, careful attention to proper collimation will exclude them from the primary beam in most examinations. Conversely, the ovaries lie within the area that the primary beam must traverse for a number of common examinations. Shielding them without loss of needed diagnostic information may require considerable ingenuity and is frequently impracticable.

Gonadal shielding is new to most patients. It may not be readily accepted. To the patient, the use of a shield implies that there is danger to his or her reproductive system in the examination. Such apprehension can be very difficult to allay, and patients may refuse examinations that are urgently needed for their immediate health benefit. It is important, although not always easy, to convey the concept that the exposure hazard to the individual is statistically negligible, but that protection is indicated because of the millions of exposures sustained by the genetic pool of the species.

G. *FILMS AND SCREENS*

Nearly all x-ray examinations other than those of extremities are made with intensifying screens, which are placed in contact with the film. The x-ray beam causes the fluorescent crystals of the screen to emit light. As much as 95 percent of the darkening of the film may result from light produced by the screens.

Manufacturers of films and screens offer a wide range of sensitivities. In general, the most sensitive systems are leasable to record fine detail. A film-screen combination should be chosen for the type of examinations to be conducted to combine detail rendition and sensitivity required for optimum information content. Screens should be kept free of dirt and scratches.

H. *FILM PROCESSING*

Even the best x-ray equipment, carefully used, will not produce satisfactory radiographs unless the darkroom equipment and techniques are comparable in quality and precision. The darkroom should be planned with the same care as the x-ray facility. It should be inspected for light leaks following construction and periodically thereafter. Proper temperature control of the processing solutions is essential. Storage of solutions should be planned to avoid contamination. Unexposed film should be checked periodically for fogging. The presence of fogging may indicate excessive age or a need for greater protection from light, heat, certain fumes, or radiation during storage. The safelight should be carefully chosen to match the film manufacturer's specifications and should be used only with a lamp of the specified wattage.

Manufacturers of x-ray films provide processing instructions and recommend suitable chemicals. The processing solutions should be kept fresh and maintained at adequate strength. Their temperature should be regulated as recommended; in general, manufacturers recommendations and technique charts should be followed. Experienced technical representatives routinely check darkroom solutions and procedures as possible causes of poor radiographs before examining the x-ray machines and controls.

I. *TECHNIQUES FOR EXAMINATIONS*

Technique charts for proper exposure of the radiographs should be obtained and followed carefully. The use of an automatic exposure timer is helpful in improving the quality of films and in reducing the number of repeat examinations.

When the film is developed and dried, it should be displayed on a view box with sufficient brightness to permit observation of fine detail. Viewing in a partially darkened room enhances perception of details. A high-intensity light is necessary for examining dark areas of the radiograph.

J. *INTERPRETATION*

The ultimate value of a radiographic examination to the patient necessarily depends upon the skill with which it is interpreted. Radiographic interpretation is the subject of many textbooks, and its study is a lifelong career for some physicians. Discussion of interpretative technique is beyond the scope of this manual; however, consultation is appropriate in any radiological examination. Radiologists, or other physicians, may be called upon to review radiographs. Better still, when feasible, the initial consultation should precede the examination for guidance in the selection of techniques for the particular clinical problem.

GLOSSARY OF RADIOLOGIC TECHNOLOGY

CONTENTS

	Page
1. ABBREVIATIONS	1
2. PREFIXES	2
3. SUFFIXES	3
4. PHYSICAL, RADIOLOGICAL, AND MEDICAL TERMS	3
ABDUCT .... AIR-DOSE	3
ALPHA RAYS .... AURICULAR POINT	4
AUTOTRANSFORMER .... CATHETER	5
CATHODE .... CONE	6
CONTRAST .... DILATION	7
DIRECT CURRENT .... ENTERIC	8
EPICONDYLE .... FREQUENCY	9
FRILLING .... INFEROSUPERIOR	10
INFRA-ORBITAL MARGIN .... LUMEN	11
MAGNET .... NAVICULAR	12
NEGATIVE CHARGE .... PASS BOX	13
PATELLA .... POTTER-BUCKY DIAPHRAM	14
PRIMARY FACTORS .... RESPIRATION	15
RESTRAINER .... SIALOGRAPHY	16
SINE WAVE .... TARGET	17
TARGET-SKIN DISTANCE .... UTERUS	18
VACUUM TUBE .... ZYGOMA	19

GLOSSARY

1. Abbreviations:

A, amp: ampere
Å: Angstrom unit
AC: alternating current
ADR: air dose rate
AP: anteroposterior
APLO: anteroposterior lateral oblique
APMO: anteroposterior medial oblique
ARS: acute radiation syndrome
ASIS: anterior superior iliac spine
AWG: American Wire Gage
B.E.: barium enema
BSF: backscatter factor
Ci: curie
cm: centimeter(s)
CR: central ray
DC: direct current
DNA: deoxyribonucleic acid
dps: disintegrations per second
DPT: double-part thickness
EAM: external auditory meatus
EFS: effective focal spot
EMF: electromotive force
EOP: external occipital protuberance
eV: electron volts
FFD: focal-film distance, focus-film distance
FRC: Federal Radiation Council
FS: focal spot
FSD: focal spot distance
GB: gallbladder
GCD: greatest common divisor
GI or G.I.: gastrointestinal
G.U.: genitourinary
H.U.: heat units
HVL: half-value layer
Hz: hertz
ICRP: International Commission on Radiation Protection
ICRU: International Commission on Radiation Units and Measurement
I.M.: intramuscular
I.V.: intravenous
IVC: intravenous cholangiogram, inferior vena cavagram
IVP: intravenous pyelogram
IOML: infra-orbitomeatal line
KeV: kilo electron volts (one thousand electron volts)
kHz: kilohertz, 1000 hertz
KUB: kidneys, ureters, and bladder
kV: Kilovolts
kVp: Kilovoltage peak
kW: kilowatt
LAO: left anterior oblique
Lat: lateral
LCD: least common divisor
LCM: least common multiple
LD: lethal dose
LPO: left posterior oblique
mA: milliampere, milliamperage
mAs: milliampere second
MeV: million electron volts
MHz: million hertz
mm: millimeter(s)
MPD: maximum permissible dose
MΩ: megohm, 1000 ohms
μCi: microcurie
μV: microvolt
mV: millivolt
NCRP: National Council on Radiation Protection and Measurements
Obl: oblique
OFD: object-film distance
OML: orbitomeatal line
PA: posteroanterior
PALO: posteroanterior lateral oblique
PAMO: posteroanterior medial oblique
P-B: Potter-Bucky
PE: photographic effect
PF: photofluorography
PFD: part-film distance
PFX: photofluorographic X-ray
PHT: primary circuit of the high-tension circuit
PSIS: posterior superior iliac spine
R: roentgen
rad: radiation absorbed dose
RAO: right anterior oblique
RBE: relative biological effectiveness
rem: roentgen equivalent man
rep: roentgen equivalent physical
r-m-s: root-mean-square value
RNA: ribonucleic acid
rpm: revolutions per minute
RPO: right posterior oblique
RR: remnant radiation
SB: small bowel
SDR: skin-dose rate
sec: second(s)
SHT: secondary circuit of the high-tension circuit
SMV: submentovertex, submentovertical
SR: secondary and scattered radiation
TFD: target-film distance
TMJ: temporomandibular joint
TSD: target-skin distance
UGI or U.G.I.: upper gastrointestinal
U.S.P.: United States Pharmacopeia
V: volts
VPT: volts-per-turn ratio
W: watt

2. Prefixes:

a or an	without, not, absence of.
ad	to, toward.
adeno	of or pertaining to a gland.
ambi or amphi	both; pertaining to or affecting both sides.
angio	pertaining to a blood vessel.
ante	before.
antero	in front of, front.
anti	opposite, against, counter.
ap or apo	separation or derivation from.
arterio	pertaining to the arteries.
bi or di	two or twice.
bio	life.
cardio	pertaining to the heart.
cephalo	pertaining to the head or skull.
cerebro	pertaining to the brain.
chiro	hand.
chole	pertaining to bile or to the biliary tract.
co	with, together.
colo	pertaining to the colon.
con	with.
costo	rib.
cysto	cyst, sac, or bladder.
dactylo	finger, toe, digit.
derma or dermato	skin.
dextro	of, pertaining to, or toward the right.
di	twice
dia	through or apart.
dis	reversal or separation.
dys	difficult, painful or bad.
ec, ecto, ex	out or out of; without, on the outer side, external, away from.
en	in, within.
encephalo	pertaining to the brain.
endo or ento	innermost, within.
entero	pertaining to the intestines.
epi	on, upon, above.
extra or extro	on the outside, beyond, in addition.
gastro	pertaining to the stomach.
hema, hemato, hemo	pertaining to the blood.
hemi	one-half; pertaining to or affecting one side of the body.
hetero	different.
homo	the same.
hydro	water.
hyper	above, beyond, or excessive.
hypno	sleep.
hypo	beneath, under, or deficient.
hystero	uterus.
ileo	ileum.
in, il, im, ir	not, in, within, inward, into, toward.
infra	beneath.
inter	between.
intra	within, inside of.
iso	equal, alike, or the same.
kilo	one thousand.
latero	to the side of.
leuko	white or colorless.
levo	of, pertaining to, or toward the left.
litho	stone or rock.
macro	large; abnormal size.
mal	bad, abnormal.
mega	great size, one million times.
melano	black.
meso	middle.
meta	change, after or next.
micro	small, one-millionth of.
mono	one or single.
morpho	form.
multi	many.
myelo	bone marrow or spinal cord.
myo	muscle.
neo	new, recent, young.
nephr, nephro	kidney.
neur, neuro	nerve.
ob	in front of, against.
odonto	tooth.
ophthalmo	eye.
ortho	straight, normal, correct.
osteo	bone.

oto	ear.
pan	all.
para	beside, alongside of, apart from.
peri	around, about.
pneumo	lung, air, or respiration.
pod, podo	foot.
poly	many, much.
post	after.
postero	behind.
prae, pre	before.
pro	before or in front of.
proct, procto	rectum.
pseudo	false.
pyo	pus.
pyr, pyro	fire or heat.
retro	backward, located behind, or against the natural course.
rhin, rhino	nose.
semi	half.
sphygmo	pulse.
sub	under, beneath.
super, supra	excess of, above, upon.
sym, syn	with, together, same.
ter, tri	three, thrice, threefold.
trans	across, through, over.
uni	one.
uro	pertaining to urine or to the urinary tract.

3. Suffixes:

agogue	inducing agent.
agra	seizure of acute pain.
algia	painful condition.
cele	tumor or swelling.
ectomy	excision.
graph	a record.
ia	disease condition.
itis	inflammation.
logy	science of.
mania	excessive preoccupation with something.
meter	instrument for measuring.
oid	like, resembling.
oma	tumor.
opia	eye or vision.
osis	fullness, redundancy, excess.
pathy	a morbid condition or disease.
phobia	morbid or exaggerated fear or dread.
plasty	plastic surgery.
rrhea	flow or discharge.
scope	instrument for making a visual examination.
scopy	visual examination.
stomy	surgical creation of an artificial opening.
tomy	incision.

4. Physical, Radiological, and Medical Terms:

Abduct. To draw away from the midline of the body; opposit of adduct.

Absorption. The attenuation or reduction in intensity of X-rays as they pass through any absorbing material. A condition in which a liquid or gas is taken up by and fills the interstitial spaces of a porous substance.

Acanthiomeatal Line. An imaginary line extending from the acanthion to the external auditory meatus.

Acanthion. A point at the base of the anterior nasal spine.

Acetabulum. The hip socket of the innominate bone.

Acromion. The outward extension of the spine of the scapula, forming the point of the shoulder.

Actual Focal Spot. The area on the X-ray tube target which is bombarded by high speed electrons and from which the X-rays are emitted.

Added Filter. A filter, usually of aluminum, designed to be placed in the portal of the tube housing for additional filtration. It filters out the softer rays and reduces the amount of radiation to the patient's skin.

Adduct. To draw toward the midline of the body; opposite of abduct.

Adipose. Fat; fatty.

Afferent. Leading into or toward an organ, tissue or collection center; opposite of efferent.

Air-Dose. The dose of radiation in roentgens measured in free air.

Alpha Rays. The positively charged particles (helium atom nuclei) which are ejected from the nucleus of certain radioactive atoms.

Alternating Current. A current in which the electrons are periodically reversing direction and speed. Ordinary United States alternating current has 60 cycles per second.

Alternation. One-half cycle of alternating current; one alternation lasts 1/120 second. Also called an impulse or pulsation.

Ambient Temperature. The temperature of the air surrounding the heated parts of an electric circuit.

Ammeter. An electrical instrument which measures current flow in amperes.

Ampere. The practical unit of measurement of electric current, indicating the rate (quantity per second) of electron flow through a conductor. One ampere equals 6.28×10^{18} electrons per second.

Angiography. The radiographic examination of the blood vascular system after the injection of an aqueous solution of contrast medium.

Angstrom. The unit of length used for measuring wavelengths of X-rays and other forms of electromagnetic waves. One angstrom equals one one-hundred millionth of a centimeter.

Anode. The positively charged portion of any vacuum tube. In the X-ray tube, the anode contains the target which is bombarded by electrons during X-ray production.

Anode Thermal Capacity. The quantitative ability of the anode portion of the X-ray tube to store and withstand large amounts of heat.

Anterior. Refers to the front portion of the body, or of an organ or part.

Anteroposterior. The positioning of a part so that the CR enters from the anterior aspect and emerges from the posterior aspect.

Antiseptic. A substance that will prohibit the growth of microorganisms without necessarily destroying them.

Antrum. A cavity or chamber, especially one within a bone.

Aorta. The large artery which carries the blood away from the heart.

Apex. The top or pointed end of any conical structure or part, as in the heart or lung.

Apnea. Temporary arrest of respiration.

Arachnoid. Resembling a spider's web.

Armature. The part of a generator or motor that rotates between the field poles and carrying windings in which the electromotive force acts for operating the machine.

Armature Coil. A coil of wire placed on the armature of a generator or motor; part of the armature winding.

Armature Core. The iron cylinder or ring on which, or in which, armature windings are carried.

Arteriography. The radiographic examination of the arteries after the injection of a contrast material.

Arthrography. The radiographic examination of a joint after injection of a contrast material.

Articular. Pertaining to a joint.

Articulation. The place of junction between two or more bones; also called joint.

Artifacts. Foreign or artificial marks on a radiograph which may be caused by static, dirty or damaged screens, loose foreign bodies in the cassette, et cetera.

Aseptic. Free from mircroorganisms which produce putrefaction or rotting.

Aspirate. The act of removing or drawing off by suction, the removal of fluids or gases from a cavity by means of an aspirator.

Atom. The smallest unit of matter which can remain unchanged in chemical reactions.

Atomic Number. The number denoting the total number of protons in the nucleus of an atom; symbol Z.

Atomic Weight. The average relative weight of an atom as compared to the weight of carbon which is represented as 12. It is approximately equal to the sum of all protons and neutrons in the nucleus of the atom; symbol A.

Atrium. A chamber affording entrance to another structure or organ; for example, one of the receiving chambers of the heart.

Attraction. The effect between magnetized bodies, as that between a magnet and iron or steel, by which they are drawn together.

Atypical. Irregular; deviating from the usual or normal.

Auricular Point. The center of the opening of the external auditory meatus.

Autotransformer. A transformer in which part of the winding is in both the primary circuit and the secondary circuit, used to boost or reduce line voltage for voltage corrections, control, et cetera; a transformer in which the primary and secondary are combined.

Axial. Derived from the term *axis* and referring to structures located symmetrically around a straight line or central point.

Axilla. The armpit, or the cavity beneath the junction of the arm and shoulder.

Axis. Any lengthwise central line, real or imaginary, around which parts of a body are symmetrically arranged, as the spinal column in man. Also, the second cervical vertebra.

Backscatter Rays. Secondary rays formed from remnant radiation which has passed through the film holder and is scattered back toward the X-ray film.

Ballistic Milliammeter. A milliammeter having a weighted needle and which measures the product of milliamperes (mA) and time (sec), and is designed to read in milliampere-seconds (mAs). See *mAs meter*.

Barium. A metallic element. The term barium is usually used to refer to barium sulfate, an insoluble compound of barium and sulfuric acid, which is used as a contrast medium in medical radiography because of its high radiopacity.

Basilar. Pertaining to a base or basal part.

Beta Rays. Charged particles (electrons or positrons) which are ejected from the nuclei of certain radioactive atoms.

Bicipital. Having two heads.

Bifurcate. To divide into two branches.

Bilateral. Having two sides; pertaining to both sides; occurring on both sides.

Biliary. Pertaining to the secretion of the liver (bile), the bile ducts, or the gallbladder.

Bregma. A topographical point on the skull at the junction of the coronal and sagittal sutures.

Bremsstrahlung. A German word, meaning "braking radiation," which is used to designate those X-rays which are formed as a result of high speed electrons being braked to a much slower speed. Bremsstrahlung may be of any wavelength up to the maximum energy of the electrons.

Bronchography. The radiographic examination of the bronchial tree using a liquid contrast medium.

Bucky (Potter-Bucky Diaphragm). A device containing a moving grid and which is placed between the patient and the film to reduce the fogging effect of secondary radiation on the radiograph. See *Grid*.

Bursa. A small sack or saclike cavity filled with fluid interposed between parts that move upon one another to prevent friction.

Calcaneus. The heel bone; also called os calcis.

Calculus. Any abnormal concentration of mineral salts within the body. Commonly called "stones."

Calibration. The process of measuring the actual output of a machine as compared to its indicated or metered output.

Canaliculus. An extremely narrow tubular passage or channel (lit. "little canal").

Cannula. A tube for insertion into a body opening.

Canthomeatal Line. See *Orbitomeatal Line*.

Canthus. The angle at either end of the slit between the eyelids; the canthi are distinguished as outer or temporal and inner or nasal.

Capacity. A general term referring to the maximum output of a machine or to the ability that a device possesses to sustain a load.

Capitulum. An eminence on the distal end of the humerus articulating with the radius.

Cardboard Holder (Direct Exposure Holder). A lighttight device for holding film for direct X-ray exposure without the use of intensifying screens.

Cardiac. Pertaining to the heart or to the end of the stomach nearest the heart.

Cardio-angiography. The radiographic examination of the heart and great vessels after intravenous injection of an aqueous solution of contrast medium. Also, referred to as angiography, angiocardiography.

Cassette. A device for holding X-ray film during exposure. It is composed of two fluorescing intensifying screens in a metal and bakelite holder.

Cassette Changer. A piece of radiographic equipment designed for quick changing of cassettes so that successive exposures may be made without changing the position of the patient, as in stereoscopy.

Catheter. A thin tube used for draining fluid from cavities or for distending passages.

Cathode. The negatively charged electrode of any vacuum tube. In the X-ray tube, the cathode contains the filament, which, when heated, produces a cloud of electrons that may be pushed across the tube to produce X-rays.

Cathode Rays. The stream of electrons flowing away from the cathode in a vacuum tube.

Caudad. Toward the tail or the lower portion of the body.

Centigrade. Temperature scale having 100 degrees of graduation, and in which 0° represents the freezing point and 100° the boiling point of water under standard conditions (sea level).

Centimeter. A unit of measurement equal to approximately 0.4 inch.

Central Ray. The theoretical center of the X-ray beam. The central ray leaves the focal spot at 90° from the long axis of the tube housing. Also called principal ray.

Cephalad. Toward the head.

Cephalic. Of or pertaining to the head.

Cephalometry. Measurement of the fetal head in the uterus.

Cerebral Angiography. The radiographic examination of the opacified blood vessels of the brain.

Cervical. Pertaining to the neck or cervical vertebrae; also, to any necklike part.

Cervix. Neck; referring to the neck of the body, or the constricted portion of an organ; for example, the cervix (neck) of the uterus.

Characteristic Radiation. X-rays which are produced by interorbital shifts of electrons within an atom. These rays are characteristic in wavelength of the specific atom which produced them.

Chemical Fog. The overall density of a radiograph produced by contaminated developer or other chemicals not by light or X-rays.

Choke Coil. A device consisting of a coil of wire with an adjustable soft iron core. The choke coil is used as a voltage and current regulator.

Cholangiography. The radiographic examination of the biliary tract following intravenous injection of a suitable contrast medium. It may be performed during or following surgery.

Cholecystography. A radiographic examination of the gallbladder following oral or intravenous administration of a suitable contrast medium.

Cinefluorography. A radiographic procedure wherein motion pictures are taken of images on a fluorescent screen. Also see *Image-Intensifier Cinefluorography.*

Circuit. The complete path through which the current flows; a certain part of the complete part, such as one of its conductors.

Clavicle. The collar bone; a bone curved like the letter s, which articulates with the sternum and the scapula.

Clearing Time. Time required for the fixer to dissolve unexposed salts in X-ray film emulsion.

Closed Circuit. An electric circuit that is complete and through which current may flow when voltage is applied.

Coccyx. The "tail" bone at the caudal end of the spinal column.

Collimator. A diaphragm or other device for confining a beam of radiation within a limited area.

Commutator. A ring of copper segments insulated from each other and connected to the windings of an armature. The alternating impulses from the armature conductors are passed by the commutator into the brushes so that current flowing through any one brush is always in the same direction.

Compression Band. A broad band made of nonopaque material employed for compression and/or immobilization.

Conductance. The conducting power of a body or a circuit for electricity. When expressed in figures, conductance is the reciprocal of resistance. The unit is the mho.

Conductor. Any material which allows easy passage of an electric current through it.

Condyle. A rounded knucklelike articular process of a bone. Applied chiefly to articular prominences occurring in pairs, such as those of the femur, mandible, and the occipital bone.

Cone. A cone-shaped device placed between the X-ray tube and the patient to limit the beam of primary radiation striking the part, thus reducing the amount of secondary radiation that is formed. See *Cylinder.*

Contrast. In general terms, contrast refers to the difference in density between the highlights and shadows seen in a radiograph. Mathematically, contrast may be defined as the ratio of the greatest density to the least density on a radiograph; the larger this ratio is, the greater the contrast is said to be. See *Scale of Contrast*.

Contrast Media. Substances which are introduced into tissues or organs for the purpose of producing radiographic contrast where contrast does not normally exist.

Coracoid Process. The hooklike process which projects anteriorly from the scapula.

Coronal Plane. Any vertical plane separating the body into anterior and posterior portions; also called the frontal plane.

Cornoid Process. A beaklike projection on the upper anterior edge of the mandible; also a process on the proximal end of the ulna.

Corpus. Body.

Cortex. The outer layer of an organ or structure.

Costal. Pertaining to the ribs.

Costophrenic Angle. The angle formed by the ribs and diaphragm; this angle can be clearly seen on a posteroanterior chest radiograph.

Cranial. Pertaining to the head.

Crest. A prominent ridge of the bone.

Cricoid. The ringlike cartilage below the "Adams's apple."

Culdoscopy. Visual examination of the female pelvic organs by means of endoscopy.

Cuneiform. Shaped like a wedge.

Current. The flow of electrons from one place to another.

Cutaneous. Pertaining to the skin.

Cyanosis. Bluish discoloration of the skin resulting from a deficiency in blood oxygen.

Cycle. One complete wave of alternating current or electromagnetic wave curve. A cycle consists of two complete alternations of alternating current.

Cylinder. A cylindrically shaped device which is sometimes used in the place of a cone. A cylinder which may be extended is called an extension cylinder.

Cyst. Any sac, normal or abnormal, especially one which contains a liquid or semisolid material.

Cystitis. Inflammation of the urinary bladder.

Cystography. The radiographic examination of the urinary bladder using an aqueous solution of a contrast medium.

Cystoscope. An instrument used for visual inspection of the interior of the urinary bladder.

Decubitus. A position for radiography in which the patient is lying down and the CR is projected horizontally. The words supine, prone, or lateral are employed in conjunction to describe the particular recumbent position.

Definition. The degree of distinctness with which image details are recorded on the X-ray film. See *Detail*.

Dens. The odontoid or toothlike process on the axis (second cervical vertebra).

Density. The degree of the blackness on a radiograph.

Density Equalization Filter. A radiographic accessory device that is used when it is desirable to cause a variation of X-ray intensity across a part of varying thickness.

Depth Dose. The dose of radiation actually delivered to a point at a specified depth below the surface of the body.

Detail. The relative sharpness of the internal structures of a body as they are demonstrated on a radiograph. This sharpness is affected by geometric factors only, whereas visibility of detail may also be affected by the density, contrast, and fog which are present.

Developer. The chemical solution used to make visible the radiographic image on X-ray film.

Diaphragm. An accessory device which consists of a sheet of lead with a hole in it; as a general rule, a diaphragm is used only when a cone or cylinder is not available. Also, the musculo-membranous partition that separates the abdomen from the thorax.

Diastole. The resting stage of the beating heart.

Dilatation. Natural or artificial enlargment, expansion, or distention of a cavity, canal, or opening.

Direct Current. An electric current in which the current flows in one direction at all times, as opposed to alternating current. A direct current in which the electrons flow smoothly, without change of speed, is called a *uniform direct current;* one in which the electrons are constantly changing speed but not direction is called *pulsating direct current.*

Direct Exposure Film. A type of X-ray film which is made to be especially sensitive in manufacture to the direct action of X-rays. This type of film is designed for use in cardboard holders only.

Distal. Remote, farthest from the center, origin, or head, as, the distal end of a long bone.

Distention. Enlargement or expansion.

Distortion. Difference in size and/or shape of the radiographic image as compared with that of the part examined. When only a change of size is involved it is called *magnified distortion.* When a change of size and shape is involved, it is termed *true distortion.*

Divergent. Radiating outward from a common point; spreading apart.

Dorsal. Pertaining to the back; situated nearer the back than some point of reference. In most cases, same as posterior and opposite of ventral.

Dorsal Spine. See *Thoracic Spine.*

Dose, Absorbed. The amount of radiation measured in rads which is absorbed by the part being exposed.

Dose Exposure. See *Exposure Dose.*

Dose Rate. The dose or amount of radiation delivered per unit of time (for example, roentgens (R) per hour).

Double Focus Tube. An X-ray tube having two focal spots, one of which is smaller than the other. The smaller one is used for maximum detail, the larger one to permit greater energy to be applied to the tube.

Dry Cell. A primary electric cell using carbon and zinc for electrodes with an electrolyte of sal ammoniac and chloride of zinc carried by some absorbent material in the cell. The carbon is the positive electrode and the zinc is the negative.

Duodenal Bulb. The triangular shaped structure forming the first portion of the duodenum and which can be seen on radiographic examination of the upper gastrointestinal tract.

Duodenum. The first or proximal portion of the small intestine, so called because it is about 12 fingerbreadths in length. It extends from the pylorus to the jejunum.

Dyspnea. Difficult breathing.

Effective Focal Spot. The perpendicular projection or effective size of the actual focal spot as it is presented to the film. The x-rays leave the rectangular actual focal spot and appear to be coming from a much smaller square area. In effect, the X-rays are emitted from the square area or the effective focal spot.

Efferent. Leading out of or away from an organ, tissue or collection center; opposite of afferent.

Electromagnet. A soft iron or soft steel core magnetized by the action of current passing through a coil around the magnet. It loses most of its magnetism as soon as the flow of current is stopped.

Electromagnetic Induction. The process by which a current is caused to flow in a circuit due to a magnetic field moving through the wires of a portion of the circuit. There are three types of electromagnetic induction: Relative motion, mutual induction, and self-induction.

Electromagnetism. Magnetism which exists about a wire while it has an electric current flowing through it.

Electromotive Force. The force which drives an electric current through a conductor. It is measured in volts. See *Voltage.*

Electron. The smallest negatively charged particle of matter revolving about the positively charged nucleus of an atom. Electrons moving through a wire constitute an electric current.

Electrostatic Unit. The quantity of electrical charge equal to the charge of 2,080,000,000 electrons.

Emulsion. The X-ray and light sensitive portion of the X-ray film before processing and the portion of the film that contains the image after processing.

Encephalography. The radiographic examination of the brain after the ventricles have been filled with a suitable contrast medium.

Energy. The capacity for performing work (moving a body through a distance).

Ensiform. See *Xiphoid Process.*

Enteric. Pertaining to the intestines.

Epicondyle. A roughened eminence upon a bone above its condyle; especially, the eminences above the condyles of the humerus.

Erythema Dose. The exposure dose which is required to cause a noticeable reddening of the skin within a few days.

Esophagus. The muscular membranous canal extending from the pharynx to the stomach.

Ethmoid. Perforated with small openings like a sieve.

Ethmoid Bone. A thin cancellous bone lying between the sphenoid and frontal bones of the skull.

Eversion. Outward rotation; for example, turning the sole of the foot away from the midline thus raising the lateral border of the foot.

Excrete. To eliminate waste material.

Expiration. The act of breathing out or expelling air from the lungs; exhaling.

Exposure Dose. The amount of radiation, measured in roentgens (R), which is delivered to a specific point.

Exposure, Radiographic. The process of subjecting a sensitive film to the action of X-rays either directly or through an intermediate step using intensifying screens.

Exposure Timer. A timer mechanism on the control panel of an X-ray machine to regulate time of exposure.

Extension. The straightening out of a part.

External. Situated or occurring on the outside.

External Auditory Meatus. The external canal or opening of the ear.

External Canthus of the Eye. See *Canthus*.

External Occipital Protuberance. A prominent eminence on the posterior portion of the occipital bone. Also called the inion.

External Rotation. Rotating a part away from the median plane.

Facial Line. A straight line touching the glabella and a point at the lower border of the face.

Femur. The thigh bone, located between the hip and knee joint.

Fetography. The radiographic examination of the fetus in utero.

Fibula. The smaller of the two leg bones located between the knee and the ankle joint.

Filament. A fine threadlike coil of tungsten which is mounted in the cathode of the X-ray tube. When heated, the filament becomes a source of electrons, the light source in an incandescent lamp and the source of free electrons in an electron tube.

Film, X-ray. The medium on which the radiographic image is recorded. See *Screen-type Film*.

Filter. See *Added Filter* and *Inherent Filtration*.

Fissure. A cleft, groove or trench.

Fixer. The chemical solution (commonly called "hypo") that clears the X-ray film and hardens the emulsion.

Flexion. The act of bending, or the condition of being bent or brought together.

Fluorescence. The emission of visible light by a crystal when subjected to an activating source.

Fluorescent Screen. A sheet of radiolucent material coated with a crystalline compound which fluoresces when exposed to X-rays.

Fluoroscope. A piece of radiographic equipment including an X-ray tube and a fluorescent screen. X-rays are absorbed by the patient and the resulting shadows are studied from the glow of the fluoroscopic screen.

Fluoroscopy. The process of examining the tissues by means of a fluoroscopic screen. See also *Image Intensification*.

Focal-Film Distance. The distance from the focal spot of the X-ray tube to the film.

Focal-skin Distance. See *Target-skin Distance*.

Focal Spot. See *Actual Focal Spot* and *Effective Focal Spot*.

Fog. A supplemental density (silver deposit) that covers part or all of the film obscuring image visualization. Fog may occur as a result of exposing the film to secondary radiation, light, heat, and chemical fumes; or if outdated film is used.

Foramen. A hole or perforation; especially in a bone.

Foramen Magnum. The large opening in the base of the skull through which the spinal cord passes.

Frequency. Number of cycles per second in an alternating current or electromagnetic wave.

Frilling. Defect in a radiograph associated with separation of the emulsion from the base at the margin of the film.

Gamma Rays. Electromagnetic radiation spontaneously emitted from radioactive deposits or materials, such as radium. Their wavelengths are shorter than those of X-rays used in diagnostic radiography, and they possess great penetrating power.

Gastrointestinal Series. A series of fluoroscopic and radiographic examinations of the gastrointestinal tract, usually using barium sulfate as a contrast medium.

Gastrointestinal Tract. The esophagus, stomach, and the small and large intestines collectively.

Glabella. The anterior protuberance of the frontal bone (between the eyebrows).

Glabella-alveolar Line. An imaginary line extending from the glabella to the upper alveolus; the localization plane of the face.

Gluteal. Pertaining to the buttocks.

Gonion. Anatomical landmark, the most inferior, posterior, and lateral point on the external angle of the mandible.

Grid. A device composed of alternate thin strips of lead and a radiolucent material encased in a suitable binder placed between the patient and the radiographic film to absorb scattered and secondary radiation.

Grid Focus. The point at which all of the radiopaque strips in a grid would meet if they were extended.

Grid Radius. The distance from the grid focus to the center of the grid.

Grid Ratio. The ratio of the height of the lead strips to the distance between them (thickness of radiolucent material).

Ground. An electrical connection to the earth or the metal framework or supports of electrical parts; a wire connecting directly to the earth, usually through a gas, water, or steam line.

Grounded Circuit. A circuit completed through ground, through the earth, or the metal framework of electrical parts.

Half-Value Layer. The thickness of a homogenous filter which will reduce the intensity of the X-ray beam to one-half of its original value.

Heat Unit. An arbitrary unit of measurement of the heat produced in an X-ray tube. Heat units are electrically equivalent to watt-seconds, and are the product of kVp X mA X sec.

Hepatic. Pertaining to the liver.

Horizontal. Parallel to the horizon or ground; at right angles to the vertical.

Hot Cathode Tube. Any X-ray tube utilizing a heated cathode for its source of electrons.

"Hypo". See *Fixer*.

Hysterosalpingography. See *uterosalpingography*.

Ileum. The last portion of the small intestine.

Iliac Crest. Referring to the curving superior border of the ilium.

Iliac Spine. A small but prominent projection on the anterior surface of the ilium; spoken of as the anterior superior iliac spine.

Ilium. The hip bone or winglike portion of the innominate bone.

Image. The deposits of black metallic silver in the emulsion of the film which represent the anatomical structures of the part X-rayed.

Image Intensification. An electronic system of producing flourescent images by amplification of the brightness level so that they may be observed by means of a mirror-optical system or on a television monitor. Viewing may be done in subdued room light and dark adaptation is unnecessary.

Image-intensifier Cinefluorography. A radiographic procedure wherein a motion picture is used with an image intensification system to record a moving study of the amplified images as they occur on the output phosphor or the image-intensifier tube.

Immobilization. The act of rendering a body part immobile during a radiographic exposure.

Impulse. See *Alternation*.

Impulse Timer. An accurate timer for making fractional second exposures.

Inferior. Situated below a particular reference point.

Inferosuperior. Directed or extended from below upward.

Infra-orbital Margin. The inferior rim of a bony orbit.

Infra-orbitomeatal Line. An imaginary line extending from the lower margin of the orbit to the external auditory meatus.

Infusion. The introduction of a fluid, as saline solution, into a vein. An infusion flows in by gravity.

Inherent Filtration. That filtration which is built into the X-ray tube housing. It includes the tube window, a thin layer of oil, and the tube portal; and, usually, is equivalent to apprximately 0.5 mm of aluminum.

Inion. Anatomical landmark, the most prominent point of the external occipital protuberance.

Innominate Bone. One of the major bones of the pelvis; composed of the ilium, the ischium, and the pubis.

Inspiration. The drawing in of breath; the act of inhaling.

Insufflator. An instrument used to introduce a gas (for example, air) into a body cavity.

Intensifying Screen. A screen composed of fluorescent material, usually calcium tungstate, placed in close contact with an X-ray film to intensify the action of X-rays in radiography.

Intensity. Refers to the concentration or quantity of X-rays striking a unit of area per unit of time.

Internal Canthus of the Eye. See *Canthus.*

International Base Line. An imaginary line extending from the external canthus of the eye to the external auditory meatus.

Interpupillary Line. An imaginary line passing through the pupils of both eyes when the eyes are in a neutral position looking straight ahead.

Intravenous Pyelography. See *Pyelography, Excretory.*

Intubation. The process of introducing a tube into a hollow organ to keep a passage open.

Inverse Square Law. The statement of the relationship which exists between the intensity of radiation striking the film and the distance of the tube from the film. The intensity of radiation is inversely proportional to the square of the distance.

Inversion. Inward rotation; for example, turning the sole inward, thus raising the medial border of the foot.

Iodized Oil. A contrast medium in which an oil (poppyseed, olive, or peanut) is combined with iodine. Used as an injection for visualization of the sinuses, bronchi, et cetera.

Ionization. The process of either adding to or subtracting electrons from neutral atoms or molecules.

Ionization Chamber. An instrument for measuring the quantity of radiation in terms of the quantity of ionization produced by the radiation.

Jejunum. The second or center portion of the small intestine.

Kilovolt. A unit of electromotive force equal to 1000 volts.

Kilovolt Peak. The very highest voltage occurring at any time during an electrical cycle; the peak kilovoltage used in making any X-ray exposure.

Kilowatt. A measurement of electrical power equal to 1000 watts.

KUB. An abbreviation indicating a plain radiograph of the abdomen to study the kidneys, ureters, and urinary bladder.

Kymograph. A device for radiographically recording the range of motion of various organs, especially the chambers of the heart throughout the cardiac cycle. The method by which this is done is called kymography.

Latent Image. The invisible image produced on an exposed X-ray film by the action of X-rays or light. It is made visible by the process of development.

Lateral. Pertaining to the side; away from the midline; a positioning of the patient so that the X-ray beam passes from one side to the other.

Latitude. The range of exposure of an X-ray film permissible for a good diagnostic result.

Ligament. A band of tissue that connects bones or supports viscera.

Lithotomy Position. Position of patient on his back, with legs flexed on the thighs, thighs flexed on the belly, and abducted.

Localize. To restrict or limit to one area or part.

Lumbar Spine. The portion of the vertebral column below the thorax; the lower five vertebrae.

Lumen. The cavity or channel within a tube or hollow organ.

Magnet. A body possessing the property of magnetism which causes it to attract materials made of iron.

Magnetic Field. The space about a magnet in which its magnetic properties are present.

Malar. Pertaining to the cheek or cheek bone.

Malar Bone. The cheek bone; same as the zygoma.

Malleolus. A rounded process on either side of the ankle joint. The process at the inner side of the lower end of the tibia is termed the *inner* or medial malleolus. The process at the outer side of the lower end of the fibula is termed the *lateral* or *external malleolus*.

Mammography. The radiographic examination of the breast.

Mandible. The lower jaw bone.

Manometer. A U-shaped tube used for measuring the pressure of gases.

mAs Meter. See *Ballistic Milliammeter*.

Matrix. Background substance; in bone, intercellular substance containing calcium and phosphate salts; in blood and lymph, the fluid in which cells are suspended.

Maxilla. The upper jaw bone.

Maximum Permissible Dose. The maximum accumulated absorbed dose of radiation to which a person may be occupationally exposed. The maximum permissible dose is calculated by the following formula: MPD = 5(N-18). N = age of individual in years.

Meatus. An opening at the end of a canal; as, the external auditory meatus.

Medial. That portion of a structure or part which is nearer to the midline than some reference point; opposite of lateral.

Median Plane. An anteroposterior plane dividing the body into right and left halves; the mid-sagittal plane.

Mediastinum. The middle compartment of the chest between the lungs. It contains all the thoracic viscera except the lungs.

Meninges. The three membranes (the dura mater, arachnoid, and pia mater) that envelop the brain and spinal cord; the lining of the spinal canal and cranial cavity.

Mental Point. Anatomical landmark, the most anterior medial point of the chin.

Metacarpus. The bones of the hand.

Metatarsus. The bones of the feet.

Meter. An instrument for measurement; a measure of length in the metric system.

Milliammeter. An electrical instrument which measures milliamperes; a milliampere meter.

Milliampere. The unit of measurement of electric current equivalent to 1/1000th of an ampere.

Milliampere-Seconds. The product of time (sec) of an X-ray exposure and the milliamperage (mA) used. The mAs determines the quantity of radiation which is produced by an exposure.

Molecule. The smallest quantity of a material which can exist and retain all its chemical properties. Molecules may be chemically decomposed into atoms.

MOP-Glabella Line. An imaginary line extending from the maximum occipital point (MOP) to the glabella. Considered to be at right angles to the facial line.

Moving Grid. A grid that moves according to a preset time of exposure, or reciprocates continuously.

Mucosa. The membrane lining tubular structures, and containing gland cells that produce a slimy substance (mucus); often called the mucous membrane; for example, the lining of the G. I. tract.

Müller's Maneuver. Making a forced inspiratory effort with the nose and mouth held closed after the patient has emptied his lungs of air. See also *Valsalva's Maneuver*.

Myelin. The fatlike substance forming a sheath around certain nerve fibers.

Myelography. The radiographic examination of the spinal canal following the injection of a suitable contrast medium.

Myocardium. The middle layer of wall of the heart; literally the muscle of the heart.

Nasion. Anatomical landmark where the midsagittal plane intersects with the interpupillary line.

Nasolabial Junction. The point at which the nose and upper lip meet.

Navicular. Shaped like a boat.

Negative Charge. An electrically unbalanced condition which results when electrons are added to a neutral body. A negative charge attracts positive charges and repels other negative charges. See *Positive Charge.*

Nephrography. The radiographic examination of the parenchymal structures of the kidneys during their radiopacification by means of a contrast medium.

Neutron. An electrically neutral or uncharged particle of matter existing along with protons in the nuclei of most atoms.

Node. A small protuberance, knob or swelling.

Nomogram. A graph that enables one by the aid of a straightedge, to read off the value of a dependent variable, when the value of the independent variable is given.

Nonopaque. Radiolucent or penetrable by X-rays.

Nucleus. The heavy centrally located portion of the atom, containing most of the weight of the atom and carrying a positive charge.

Object-Film Distance. See *Part-film Distance.*

Oblique. Refers to a part having been rotated or turned less than 90° with respect to the X-ray film and the tube.

Occipital Bone. The bone that forms the base of the skull, posteriorly.

Occiput. The back of the head.

Odontoid Process. The toothlike process situated on the second cervical vertebra (axis) for articulation with the first cervical vertebra (atlas).

Ohm. The unit for designating electrical resistance.

Ohm's Law. The relationship between voltage (E), current (I), and the resistance (R) in an electrical circuit, and which may be expressed as: $E + I \times R$.

Oil Transformer. A transformer which is insulated by a bath of oil which circulates and cools the heated parts of the transformer while acting as an insulator.

Olecranon. The large bony process at the proximal end of the ulna; commonly called the elbow.

Opaque. Impenetrable by light or X-rays in the diagnostic quality range. Opposite of nonopaque and radiolucent.

Opaque Media. Any contrast media which may be introduced into a body cavity or structure to render it radiopaque to X-rays.

Open Circuit. An incomplete circuit, one broken at any point, so that current does not flow through any part of it.

Optimum kVp. A technique of exposure using a fixed kVp, as opposed to variable kVp.

Orbit. The path in which a body moves as it rotates about another body which attracts it. Also, the bony cavity containing the eye.

Orbitomeatal Line. An imaginary line extending from the external canthus to the external auditory meatus, and used in radiography for localization purposes. It is often called the canthomeatal line. NOT to be confused with the acanthiomeatal line.

Orifice. The entrance or outlet of any body cavity, or tube.

Orthoradiography. An examination minimizing distortion to record a part in its actual size.

Os Calcis. See *Calcaneus.*

Osseous. Of or pertaining to bone.

Ossicle. A small bone.

Overexposure. The result of exposing an X-ray film or person to an excessive amount of X-rays.

Oxidation. The process of changing a compound by removing one or more electrons from an atom, ion, or molecule. Oxidation signifies the loss of an electron.

Palmar. Referring to the palm of the hand.

Parallel. Lying evenly everywhere in the same direction but never meeting, however far extended; running side by side.

Paranasal Sinuses. The accessory sinuses which communicate with the nasal passages: the ethmoid, the frontal, the maxillary, and the sphenoid.

Parietal Bones. The large bones on either side of the top of the cranium. They form the greater part of the top, sides and roof of the skull.

Part-Film Distance. The distance between the X-ray film and the part being examined.

Part-thickness. The measurement, usually in centimeters, of the part being examined.

Pass Box. A two-way, lighttight tunnel for passing exposed and unexposed films in cassettes between the darkroom and exposure rooms. Also called transfer cabinet.

Patella. The knee cap.

Pelvimetry. Measurement of the dimensions and capacity of the female pelvis by radiographic methods.

Pelvis. The bony ring at the posterior extremity of the trunk, supporting the spinal column and resting upon the lower extremities. It is composed of the two innominate bones at the sides and in front, and the sacrum and coccyx behind.

Penetration. Refers to the ability of X-rays to pass through materials.

Percutaneous. Performed through the skin.

Perfusion. A liquid poured over or through something; the introduction of fluids into the tissues by their injection into the arteries.

Pericardium. The membranous sac that contains the heart and first portion of the great vessels.

Periphery. The outer surface or the circumference of a part of the body.

Perirenal Insufflation. Radiographic examination of the kidneys by air insufflation.

Peristalsis. Waves of contractions which pass along tubular organs and move the contents forward. Usually applied to the gastrointestinal tract.

Peritoneum. The serous membrane which lines the abdominal wall and invests the viscera.

Permissible Dose. See *Maximum Permissible Dose.*

Perpendicular. Of or pertaining to any two lines which meet at right angles.

Petrous Bone. The dense pyramidal-shaped portion of the temporal bone which houses the auditory canal.

Phalanges. The fourteen bones of the fingers and the toes.

Phosphorescence. The emission of light by a crystal after the activating source has ceased.

Photofluorography. The radiographic procedure by which a photograph is taken of a fluorescent image on a fluorescent screen. Also called photoroentgenography.

Photon. An individual electromagnetic ray; a "bundle" or "packet" of electromagnetic energy (quantum) that travels at the speed of light. Same as a quantum.

Phrenic. Pertaining to the diaphragm.

Pi Lines. Lines formed on film during automatic processing which were not intended to appear on the finished radiograph.

Placentography. Radiographic examination of the walls of the uterus for localization of the placenta.

Plantar. Pertaining to the sole of the foot.

Pleura. The serous-membrane cover of the lungs which lines the thoracic cavity and encloses the potential space called the pleural cavity.

Pneumoarthrography. Injection of air as a contrast medium into a joint space for the purpose of visualizing cartilaginous structures radiographically.

Pneumoencephalography. The radiographic examination of the ventricles of the brain after removal of varying amounts of cerebrospinal fluid and replacing it with air as a contrast medium.

Pneumoperitoneography. The radiographic examination of the peritoneum and intra-abdominal organs by means of an injection of air as a contrast medium.

Pneumothorax. The presence of air or gas in the pleural cavity may occur spontaneously or be caused by trauma.

Popliteal. Pertaining to the posterior surface of the knee.

Positive Charge. That electric charge which is left when electrons are removed from a neutral body. A positive charge attracts negative charges but repels other positive charges. See *Negative charge.*

Posterior. Toward the back (or dorsal surface) of the body.

Posteroanterior. The positioning of a part so that the CR enters its posterior aspect and exists from its anterior aspect.

Post-evacuation Film. A film of the large bowel made after the patient has evacuated the contrast medium.

Potential Difference. The difference in electrical pressure or voltages between two points in a circuit.

Potter-Bucky Diaphragm. See *Bucky.*

Primary. The part of any electrical device or circuit, attached directly to the source, as distinguished from the secondary which means parts depending directly on the primary in place of the source. Also a source that produces electricity for further action such as mechanical or chemical action.

Primary Factors. The primary radiographic factors to be considered when making an X-ray exposure are (1) kilovolt peak (kVp); (2) milliamperage (mA); (3) exposure time (sec); and (4) focal-film distance (FFD). These four primary factors can be adjusted on an X-ray machine to control the quality and quantity of radiation striking the film.

Primary Radiation. The X-rays which emanate directly from the actual focal spot of the X-ray tube.

Process. A projection, especially on a bone.

Pronation. Turning downward; applied to the hand, turning the palm downward; applied to the foot, lowering the medial margin of the foot.

Prone. A position of the body lying face downward.

Prostatography. The radiographic examination of the prostate gland.

Proton. The subatomic particle found within the nucleus of an atom. The proton is the unit of positive electrical charge.

Proximal. Nearer the point of attachment or origin.

Psoas Muscles. The heavy muscles of the lower spine.

Psoas Shadows. The radiographic appearance of the psoas muscles, which are pyramidal in shape, extending downward on either side of the spinal column from the 12th dorsal vertebra to the level of the iliac crest.

Pulmonary. Pertaining to the lungs.

Pulsating. Occurring in rhythmic beats or surges; for example, the pulsating current in an X-ray tube.

Pulsation. See *Alternation.*

Pyelography, Excretory. The radiographic examination of the kidneys, pelves, and ureters after the intravenous injection of a contrast medium which passes quickly into the urine. Also called intravenous pyelography (IVP).

Pylorus. The orifice between the termination of the stomach and the duodenal bulb.

Quantum. One of the very small increments into which many forms of energy are subdivided.

Radiation. Any kind of particle or wave which leaves a point source and radiates outward in all directions. Light and X-rays are forms of radiation.

Radiation Absorbed Dose. The unit of absorbed radiation dose equal to 100 ergs of energy absorbed per 1 gram of absorbing tissue.

Radioactive. A term referring to atoms which have unstable nuclei. As these atoms change to a more stable form they emit energy from the nucleus as alpha rays, beta rays, or gamma rays.

Radiograph. The record on a film which represents anatomical details of the part examined and which is formed by the differential absorption of X-rays within the part.

Radiography. The use of X-rays in making radiographs for diagnostic interpretation.

Radiologist. A physician who uses all forms of radiation in the diagnosis and treatment of disease.

Radiology. The science which deals with the use of all forms of radiant energy in the diagnosis and treatment of disease.

Radiolucent. That property of a material which allows it to be readily penetrated by X-rays.

Radiopaque. That property of a material which causes it to absorb a relatively large amount of the X-rays passing through it.

Radius. A straight line extending from the center to the periphery of a circle. Also, the bone of the lateral aspect of the forearm.

Ratio of Transformer. The ratio of the number of turns in the primary winding of a transformer to the number of turns in the secondary winding.

Rectification. The process of changing alternating current into pulsating direct current. See *Direct Current.*

Rectifier. A device which is used to rectify alternating current.

Recumbent. Lying down or reclining.

Reduction. The process of changing a compound by adding one or more electrons to an atom, ion, or molecule. Reduction signifies the gain of an electron.

Renal. Pertaining to the kidney.

Resistance. The opposition offered by a substance or body to the passage through it of an electric current, which is measured in ohms.

Respiration. The process of breathing.

Restrainer. In radiography, a chemical employed to check development of the unexposed silver bromide and to control the working speed of the developer with respect to the exposed silver bromide.

Reticular. Having the appearance of a network.

Retrograde. Back or directed against the natural course or flow.

Retrograde Pyelography. The radiographic examination of the urinary tract in which the contrast medium is injected into the pelves of the kidneys through catheters which are inserted into the ureters. Also called retrograde urography.

Roentgen. The unit of radiologic exposure dose designated by the symbol "R". One "R" of exposure will produce in tissues an absorbed dose of approximately one rad. The roentgen, rad and rem may be considered equivalent for purposes of X-ray protection.

Roentgen Rays. X-rays.

Rotating Anode Tube. An X-ray tube in which the target constantly rotates during exposure, thus permitting the heat to be distributed over a much larger area with a corresponding increase in X-ray producing capacity.

Rotation. The movement of a part about its axis.

Ruga. A ridge or fold of the mucous membrane, found in the palate, the stomach and vagina.

Sacrum. A curved triangular bone composed of five united vertebrae, situated between the fifth lumbar vertebra above and the coccyx below and the innominates on each side, and forming the posterior boundary of the pelvis.

Sagittal Plane. A plane which divides the body into right and left portions (not necessarily equal); of, or pertaining to the sagittal suture of the cranium which lies in the median plane of the body.

Salpingography. The radiographic examination of the fallopian tubes following injection of a suitable contrast medium.

Scale of Contrast. The range of densities in a radiographic image; the number of shades of gray demonstrated on the film. In general, a long scale of contrast (many shades of gray) is also a low contrast, while a short scale of contrast (few shades of gray-black against white) is also a high contrast. See Contrast.

Scanography. A method of orthoradiography for measuring the length of long bones.

Scapula. The shoulder blade; a flat, triangular shaped bone forming the posterior aspect of the shoulder girdle.

Scattered Radiation. Those rays that have suffered a change in direction after collision with interposed material.

Scout Film. A preliminary or survey film of a part, usually taken prior to the administration of opaque media; also to check technical factors.

Screen. A device consisting of a rigid backing on which fluorescent crystals are coated. A term applied both to a fluoroscopic screen and an intensifying screen.

Screen-type Film. A film having an emulsion which is designed to be especially sensitive to the bluish light emitted from intensifying screens. It may also be used in cardboard holders but, if so, requires more exposure than *direct exposure film.*

Secondary Factors. The factors which describe the quality of a finished radiograph. These are: density, contrast, detail, and distortion.

Secondary Radiation. X-rays which are produced as the result of the interaction of primary radiation and the absorbing material of the part being examined. Secondary rays go in all directions and may produce an overall density (fog) on the film.

Sella Turcica. A saddle-shaped bone structure at the base of the skull, in the sphenoid bone, which holds the pituitary gland.

Septum. A dividing wall; a partition.

Serial Films. A series of exposures taken to record progressive events; may also refer to films made at specified intervals for small bowel studies.

Serialography. A radiographic technique for making multiple exposures of a part or organ on a single film.

Serrated. Having a sawlike edge.

Short Circuit. An accidental connection of low resistance between the two sides of a circuit so that little or no current flows through the current-consuming device in the circuit.

Sialography. The radiographic examination of the salivary glands and ducts after the injection of a suitable contrast medium.

Sine Wave. A mathematical curve which is used to diagrammatically represent the flow of an alternating current or the change in magnetic and electric fields of electromagnetic radiations.

Sinus. A hollow cavity within a bone; especially those within the face and cranium, for example, the paranasal sinuses.

Skeletal Survey. A series of radiographs taken of the whole skeleton to rule out presence of pathology.

Skeleton. The body framework of the human body consisting of 206 named bones.

Soft Tissue Radiography. A special radiographic technique to demonstrate anatomical details of soft tissue.

Spectrum. A series of electromagnetic radiations arranged in the order of their wavelengths.

Sphenoid Bone. Irregular wedge-shaped bone at the base of the skull.

Sphincter. A ringlike band of muscle fibers which closes a natural orifice.

Sphygmomanometer. A device for measuring blood pressure.

Spinal Fluid. Fluid in the spinal canal surrounding the spinal cord.

Spine. The vertebrae composing the backbone or vertebral (spinal) column. Also, a sharp projection on a bone.

Spinning Top Test. To check an X-ray timer by means of a rotating circular metallic disc with a perforation at its periphery.

Spinous Process. That part of a vertebra which projects backward from the arch, giving attachment to muscles.

Splenoportography. The radiographic examination of the venous circulation in the spleen and related blood channels following introduction of a contrast medium.

Spot Film. A radiograph made of small isolated areas during fluoroscopy.

Stasis. A standing still or stoppage of the normal flow of the contents of the vessels or of any organ of the body.

Static Marks. Artifacts produced on a film due to discharges of static electricity. They may appear as irregularly shaped lines resembling trees, streaks, or smudges.

Stationary Gird. A thin wafer grid placed between the cassette and the part to be examined in order to absorb secondary and scattered radiation.

Stenosis. Narrowing or stricture of a duct or canal.

Step-up or Step-down Transformers. See *Transformer.*

Stereoradiography. The radiographic procedure by which two films are exposed of the same part from slightly different tube positions without moving the patient. The films so produced are then viewed on a stereoscopic viewing box in order to obtain a third dimensional effect not visible on the plain radiograph. Also called stereoscopy.

Sternal Angle. The angle formed by the junction of the manubrium and the gladiolus or body of the sternum. Also called Angle of Louis.

Sternum. The breast bone; it consists of three portions, the manubrium, the gladiolus, and the xiphoid (ensiform) process.

Stop Bath. An acid solution into which film may be immersed before fixing in order to stop the developing action promptly.

Storage Capacity. A term referring to the maximum quantity of heat measured in heat units which may be stored within an X-ray tube without burning out the tube.

Subcutaneous. Beneath the skin, hypodermic.

Submentovertex. The positioning of the head and X-ray tube so that the CR ray enters at a point just below the symphysis mentis and exists from the top or crown (vertex) of the skull.

Superior. Situated above or occurring in a higher position; also referring to the upper surface of an organ or structure.

Superoinferior. Directed from above downward.

Supination. The act of or position of lying on the back. The rotation of the hand so that the palm faces upward.

Supine. Lying face up.

Symphysis. The median point or union of two paired bones; as, the symphysis pubis.

Systole. The period of the heart's contraction; also, the contraction itself.

Target. The portion of the anode of the X-ray tube against which the electron stream is directed.

Target-Skin Distance. The distance from the target of the X-ray tube to the skin; this is a necessary consideration in determining absorbed dose by a patient in radiation therapy.

Teleroentgenogram. A film, usually of the chest, made at a distance of 6 feet.

Temporal Bone. The irregular bone at the side and base of the skull containing the organs of hearing.

Temporomandibular Joint. The joint between the temporal bone and the lower jaw located just anterior to the external auditory meatus.

Therapy. A term used in radiology to indicate treatment with radium, radioactive isotopes, and/or X-rays.

Thoracic. Pertaining to, or situated in the region of the chest.

Thoracic Spine. That portion of the vertebral column to which the ribs are attached. Also called dorsal spine.

Thorax. The part of the body between the neck and diaphragm and encased by the ribs.

Tibia. The longer of the two bones of the leg. The shin bone.

Timer. The device used on an X-ray machine to complete the electrical circuit so that X-rays will be produced for a limited period of time. See *Exposure Timer* and *Impulse Timer.*

Time-temperature Development. A method of film development in which the time or duration of development is dependent upon the temperature of the developer.

Tomography. A special technique in which various selected planes of the body can be clearly demonstrated on a radiograph while structures above or below are blurred in various degrees. Also termed planigraphy, laminagraphy, stratigraphy, and body-section radiography.

Transformer. An electrical device which changes an alternating current of a given voltage and amperage into another alternating current of a different voltage and amperage. A step-down transformer decreases voltage and increases amperage. A step-up transformer increases voltage and decreases amperage.

Transverse. Crosswise; lying perpendicular to the longitudinal axis of the body.

Transverse Plane. Any plane passing through the body perpendicular to the midsagittal and coronal planes.

Transverse Processes of Vertebrae. The bony projections which extend outward on either side of a vertebra to furnish attachments for muscles.

Trendelenburg Position. A supine position in which the pelvis is higher than the head of the patient. For radiographic purposes, the body may be tilted as much as 45°.

Trephining. Removing circular disks of bone from the skull with a crown saw (trephine).

Trochanter. One of two large rounded processes on either side of the femur, just below the femoral neck. The one on the outer side is called the greater trochanter, while the one on the medial side is called the lesser trochanter.

Trochlea. A modified condyle on the distal end of the humerus.

Tubercle. A small rounded projection on a bone.

Tuberosity. A large rounded projection on a bone.

Ulna. The inner and larger bone of the forearm, on the side opposite that of the thumb.

Underexposure. The result of exposing the X-ray film to an insufficient amount of X-rays.

Ureter. A small tube which carries urine from the kidney to the bladder.

Ureterography. The radiographic examination of the ureters after the injection of a contrast medium.

Urethra. The canal through which urine is excreted from the bladder.

Urethrography. The radiographic examination of the urethra after the injection of a contrast medium.

Urography. The radiographic examination of the urinary tract, or any of its parts, after the injection of the contrast medium.

Uterosalpingography. Radiographic examination of the uterus and fallopian tubes after introduction of contrast media. Also called hysterosalpingography.

Uterus. Womb

Vacuum Tube. Any type of sealed tube which has a very low gas pressure and will allow an electric current to flow through it. X-ray tubes and valve tubes are examples of vacuum tubes.

Valsalva's Maneuver. Forced expiration against a closed glottis after the patient has taken in a deep breath.

Variable kVp. Technique of exposure using a changeable kVp, as opposed to optimum kVp.

Vena Cava. One of the great veins the purpose of which is to carry blood back to the heart. It can be visualized on angiocardiograms.

Venography. The radiographic examination of venous structures during the injection of a radiopaque solution.

Venography, Portal. The radiographic examination of the liver following injection of a contrast solution directly into the portal vein.

Ventral. Situated in front of; referring to the anterior surface of the body.

Ventriculography. The radiographic examination of the ventricular system of the brain after removing the cerebrospinal fluid through threphine holes and filling the ventricles with a contrast medium.

Vertex. The crown or top of the skull.

Vertical. Perpendicular to the plane of the horizon; upright. Also, of or pertaining to the vertex of the skull.

Verticosubmental. The positioning of the head and X-ray tube so that the central ray enters the vertex and emerges from just below the chin.

Vesicle. A small bladder or sac containing liquid.

Viscus. Any large interior organ in any one of the three great cavities of the body, especially in the abdomen.

Volt. The unit of electrical pressure or electromotive force. One volt is that amount of electrical pressure (EMF) which is required to force one ampere of current through one ohm of resistance.

Voltage. The electrical pressure which causes electricity to move measured in volts. See also *Electromotive Force* and *Potential Difference*.

Voltmeter. An instrument for measuring electromotive force in units designated as volts.

Vomer. One of the facial bones entering into the formation of the nasal septum.

Watt. The practical unit of electric power. One watt is produced when one volt pushes a current of one ampere.

Wavelength. The distance between consecutively recurring points on a sine wave.

Xiphoid Process. The small triangular bony segment forming the lower end of the sternum. Also called ensiform.

X-rays. A form of electromagnetic radiation possessing very short wavelengths and high penetrating power.

X-ray Tube. A vacuum tube which is designed especially for the purpose of producing X-rays.

Zero Potential. Having neither positive nor negative voltage or pressure.

Zygoma. Same as malar bone.

SKELETAL ANATOMY

A TABLE OF THE BONES

Contents

	Page
Head	1
Face	1
Ear	2
Neck	2
Vertebrae	2
Upper Extremities	3
Lower Extremities	4

SKELETAL ANATOMY

A TABLE OF THE BONES

NAME	PRINCIPAL FEATURES	ARTICULATION
HEAD		
OCCIPITAL (1)	Back part and base of cranium.	Parietal (2): Temporal (2) Sphenoid: Atlas.
PARIETAL (2)	Form sides and roof of skull.	Opposite Parietal; Occipital; Frontal; Temporal; Sphenoid
FRONTAL (1)	The forehead bone; and enters into formation of the orbits and nasal cavity.	Parietal (2); Sphenoid; Ethnoid; Nasal (2); Maxillary (2); Lacrimal (2); Malar (2)
TEMPORAL (2)	Situated at side and base of skull	Occipital; Parietal; Sphenoid; Inferior maxillary; Malar
SPHENOID (1)	Anterior part of base of skull, and binds the other cranial bones together.	All the cranial bones; Malar (2); Palate (2); Vomer
ETHMOID (1)	Forms part of the orbits, nasal fossae, and base of cranium.	Sphenoid; Frontal; Nasal (2); Maxillary (2); Lacrimal (2); Vomer; Palate (2)
FACE		
NASAL (2)	Form the bridge of the nose	Frontal; Ethmoid; opposite Nasal; Maxillary.
MALAR (2)	The cheek bones; form the prominence of the cheek; and part of the outer wall and floor of the orbit.	Frontal; Sphenoid; Temporal; Maxillary.
MAXILLA (2)	The upper jaw bones; assist in forming part of the floor of the orbit; the floor and outer wall of the nasal fossae; and the greater part of the roof of the mouth.	Frontal; Ethmoid; Nasal; Malar; Lacrimal; Palate; Vomer; opposite Maxilla
MANDIBLE	The lower jaw bones; serves for the reception of the lower teeth.	Temporal
LACRIMAL (2)	Situated at the front part of the inner wall of the orbit. Contain part of the canal through which the tear duct runs.	Frontal; Ethmoid; Maxillary; Inferior Turbinated

VOMER	Situated at the lower and back part of the nasal cavity; forms part of the central septum of the nose.	Sphenoid; Ethmoid; Maxillary (2); Palate (2); Septal Cartilage
PALATE (2)	Back part of nasal cavity; help to form floor and outer wall of nose, the roof of the mouth, and floor of the orbit.	Sphenoid, Ethmoid, Maxillary; Vomer; opposite Palate
INFERIOR TURBINATED	Situated in the nostril, on the outer wall of each side.	Ethmoid; Maxilla, Lacrimal; Palate
EAR MALLEUS (2) INCUS (2) STAPES (2)		
NECK HYOID	An isolated U-shaped Bone lying in front of throat; supports the tongue.	None
VERTEBRAE CERVICAL (7) THORACIC or DORSAL (12) LUMBAR (5) SACRAL (5) COCCYGEAL (4)	Each vertebra consists of two essential parts, — a ventral solid portion or body, and a dorsal portion or arch. Each arch has seven processes:- 4 articular (2 to connect with bone above, and 2 to connect with bone below); 2 transverse, one at each side; and one spinous process, projecting backwards	1. The 1st cervical vertebra, the Atlas, articulates with the occiput, supports the head. 2. The 2nd cervical vertebra, the Axis, acts as a pivot for rotating the head. 3. The different vertebrae are connected by (a) the articular processes; (b) by discs of intervertebral fibrocartilage (containing nuclear material) placed between the vertebral bodies; and (c) by broad thin ligaments called the "ligamenta flava" which connect the transverse processes. 4. The dorsal vertebrae articulate with the ribs. 5. The sacral vertebrae articulate with the ilium of the pelvis.

RIBS (12 each side)	Situated 12 on each side of thoracic cavity. The first 7 pairs are "true" ribs. The 8th, 9th, and 10th pairs are attached in front to the costal cartilages of the next rib above. The 2 lowest pairs are unattached in front and are termed "floating" ribs.	All 12 pairs are attached in back to the dorsal vertebrae. The first 7 pairs (true ribs) are connected with the Sternum in front through the costal cartilages.
STERNUM	The breastbone, situated in the median line, in front of chest. The upper part is the "manubrium", the middle and largest section is the "gladiolus" and the lowest portion is the "uniform" or "xiphoid" process.	Clavicles (2) through clavicular notches of manubrium; first 7 pairs of ribs.
UPPER EXTREMITIES CLAVICLE	Collar bone, situated horizontally above the thorax	Sternum; Scapula through clavicular facet; cartilage of 1st rib.
SCAPULA	Shoulder blade, situated between 2nd and 8th ribs on back part of thorax.	Clavicle, through acromial process of scapula; Humerus, through glenoid cavity.
HUMERUS	Upper-arm bone. Upper end consists of a rounded "head" joined to the shaft by a constricted "neck", and of two eminences, called the "greater" and "lesser Tuberosities". Lower end consists of a broad articular surface called the "trochlea" which is divided by a ridge into the internal and external condyles.	The "head" articulates with glenoid cavity of scapula. The external and internal condyles and trochlea articulate with the radius and ulna.
ULNA	Occupies the inner (little finger) side of forearm. Upper end consists of two larger curved processes and two concave cavities. The larger process is the "olecranon process"; the smaller, the "coronoid process." Between these processes is the "greater sigmoid" cavity. On the outer side of the coronoid is the "lesser sigmoid" cavity. The lower end of the ulna ends in two prominences, — an outer, or "head" and an inner, "styloid process".	The greater sigmoid cavity articulates with the trochlea of the humerus. The lesser sigmoid cavity receives the head of the radius. The lower head of the ulna articulates with the lower end of the radius. The styloid process serves for the attachment of ligaments from the wrist. The ulna does not articulate with the wrist bones.
RADIUS	Occupies the outer (thumb) side of forearm. Upper end contains a disc-shaped "head" which is shallowly depressed for articulation with the humerus, and has a prominent ridge about it, like the head of a nail, by means	See under "Principal Features" for articulation.

	of which it rotates within the lesser sigmoid cavity of the ulna. Lower end widens out on bottom to a styloid process and two smooth portions which articulate with the semilunar and scaphoid bones of the carpus.	
CARPUS (8 each hand)	The wrist bones. Are arranged in two rows; 1st row (proximal); scaphoid (or navicular), cuneiform, pisiform, semilunar; -2nd row (distal); trapizium, trapezoid, os magnum, unciform.	1st row articulates with radius, through scaphoid and semilunar bones. 2nd row articulates with metacarpal bones.
METACARPUS (5 each side)	The bones of the palm, one in line with each finger.	At their bases with each other, and with the 2nd row of carpal bones. At their heads, with the first row of phalanges.
PHALANGES	The bones of the fingers, three for each finger, and two for the thumb.	The proximal row articulates with the metacarpals, and with the second row, etc.
LOWER EXTREMITIES HIP BONE PELVIS	The two hip bones together form the sides and front wall of the pelvic cavity. Each bone has three separate parts, which unite in the adult. These parts are the "ilium", which forms the prominence of the hip, the "ischium" and the "pubis." Where these bones meet and finally unite is a deep socket, the "Acetabulum", into which the head of the femur fits. Both hip bones join at the inner margins of each pubis to form the "symphasis pubis." The sacrum articulates on either side with the inner margins of each ilium to form the "sacroiliac" joints.	Femur through glenoid cavity, Sacrum through sacroiliac joint.
FEMUR	The thigh bone. Upper end consists of a rounded head, joined to the shaft by a constricted neck, and of two eminences, the "greater" and "lesser trochanters." The lower end is divided into two large eminences, the "medial" and "external condyles", separated by an intervening notch.	"Head" articulates with the glenoid cavity of the hip bone; Patella; Tibia, through the medial and lateral semi-lunar cartilages.
PATELLA	The knee cap.	Articulates with the two condyles of the femur.

TIBIA	The shin bone, situated at the front and medial side of the leg. Upper end is large and expanded into two eminences with concave surfaces, which receive the condyles of the femur. The lower end is prolonged downward into a process called the "medial malleolus".	Articulates with the condyles of the femur, and on the lower end with the fibula and the astragalus of the tarsus.
FIBULA	Situated at outer side of leg, running parallel to tibia. Upper end has a "head" which articulates with tibia. The lower end is prolonged downward into a pointed process, the "lateral" or "external malleolus".	Articulates with the tibia above and below, and with the astragalus of the tarsus.
TARSUS (7 each foot)	The ankle bones. Consists of the Calcaneum or Os Calcis (heel bone); Astragalus; Cuboid; Scaphoid; External Cuneiform; Internal Cuneiform; and middle Cuneiform.	Astragalus articulates with Tibia and fibula. Also articulates with metatarsal bones.
METATARSUS (5 each side)	The sole or instep bones, one in line with each toe.	With the tarsal bones on one end, and the first row of toe phalanges on the other.
PHALANGES	The bones of the toes; three for each toe, and two for the great toe.	The proximal row articulates with the metatarsals, and with the second row, etc.

www.ingramcontent.com/pod-product-compliance
Lightning Source LLC
Chambersburg PA
CBHW081824300426
44116CB00014B/2477